This Journal Notebook belongs to:

_____

_____

_____

You are more capable than you think you are.
You can achieve anything that you put your mind to.
May you be happy, healthy, and well in every way.

Apple An

All-in-One Dotted Journal Notebook

For a Busy, Productive & Mindful Life

Planners + Organizers + To-dos + Reminders + Trackers + Journals + Random Notes + Doodles + Nuggets of Goodness

Apple An
(www.AppleAnBooks.com)

Copyright © 2023 by Voices Heard Publishing, LLC

All right reserved.

No part of this journal notebook may be reproduced in any form without prior written permission from the publisher.

ISBN: 978-1-958900-11-6

Voices Heard Publishing, LLC
www.VoicesHeardPublishing.com

Edition: M1.V1.P2

2023.12

Introduction

I love the magic feeling of using a pen to produce something. For many years, I used lined notebooks, used paper-based planners, post-it, loose papers, any random notebook that might be nearby, along with Google Keep and other digital apps. I struggled to keep up and be productive.

My life has improved significantly since I started using BuJo (Bullet Journal) a few years ago. Its general idea of gathering everything together in one place was appareling and effective. It allows one to be creative in their own way of journaling.

With a blank dotted notebook, I must set up my templates for my needs. It was fun initially, and I was creative about doing things differently. But as time passed, I largely stayed with a fixed set of templates. Then, preparing templates constantly on a blank page became a chore.

Since there are no journals out that would address my needs, I developed this journal notebook for myself. Each month has pre-defined, yet flexible, templates. They help me organize big goals and manage baby steps in all aspects of my life. There are also spaces for jotting, doodling, scribbling, journaling, or whatever I may be in the mood for. I want this journal notebook for everything I need to record on paper and call it my all-in-one journal assistant.

My use of the notebook allows me to be aware of myself (inside out from feelings, thoughts, and actions), my surroundings, my priorities, and thus gives me peace of mind.

I hope this book can also help those who want to live a productive and mindful life. If you feel overwhelmed by organizing your life, this notebook might be also for you.

Visit www.AppleAnBooks.com/Books/All-in-One, or scan the QR code below, for more up-to-date examples of how to use various templates and cross multiple books. On the website, you can also let me know which features you wish to have or do not use. I may incorporate them in future designs to serve more people better.

With much appreciation and best wishes to you,

Apple

Apple's Use Examples

ADVICE TO YOU: This journal notebook is to serve YOU. Own it as yours. Use it any way you like. Be creative. Have fun and be productive at the same time. Be patient when developing habits and identifying your efficiencies.

MY USES: The following filled-in pages are examples of my current uses. I continue to revise designs to meet new demands or insights. Each month can be different. Once I establish a habit or routine, I may add a new template or repurpose a current design. When using this notebook, I decide what contents to go inside each template. I can be concise with a bullet point or write long and intense. And I can be neat or messy, serious or goofy.

BOOK INDEX: This is for quick search in the future. When index a major topic/subject on a particular day, you can write down some significant matters there. For example, a long-time friend John's daughter visited unexpectedly on 11/6. A Xmas party at work happened on 12/5. An important task started on 11/30 but needed to continue later.

FUTURE LOG: The future months start from this month. The shaded areas are for decoration or writing down the months. For each month, you can use one column, three, or anyway you like. Use this template for high-level and long-term planning on critical tasks, milestones, places to travel, etc. You can use colors or highlights for individual projects over months to make them stand out.

MONTHYLY GOALS: You can plan your life in more facets than just business and personal. This template allows 13 facets. These can be work projects, business projects, family affairs, children's events, hobbies, books to read, chapters to write, parties to go, garden tasks for the season, etc. There is room for the 14th facet. You can repurpose the unused facets. I may put a sticker or a drawing there.

MONTH AT A GLANCE: Like a regular calendar, you put down things you want a quick reminder. These can be projects, milestones, deadlines, meetings, birthdays, vacations, doctors' visits, etc.

MONTHLY TRACKERS: Tracking can be effective in forming habits or building accountability and awareness. Track what you want or need to track. Each month can be different. It is okay to miss days. The vertical lines are to help group related items. Tracking examples include physical activities (hiking, running, tennis, gardening), spiritual practices (meditation, yoga), health indicators (weight, blood pressure), pets (do chickens count? I track # of eggs my girls give me), and habit forming (celery juicing, intermittent fasting). I also use a scale of 1 to 3 to track mood, physical energy, and mental sharpness.

DAILY QUOTES: I use them for gratitude, wishes and wants, or kind gestures or words for self-love and the love of others. Write two lines each day. Do not feel bad if you miss some days. You can also use these for motivational or inspirational quotes from others or from you. Another use of this template is for tracking progress in more detail (such as health recovery).

DAILY LOG: This is the most used template to keep me grounded daily. The left side has to-dos and meetings planned beforehand and check off (suggested key is at the top). The jotting space is for random or scribbling notes for doing tasks that day. They are like loose papers or post-it notes and provide a memory later for reflections or task continuation. The two hexagon shapes are for easily dividing the space for various topics. The right side allows you to note the weather of the day if that is important to you, and to write lengthy reflections of the day.

BLANK PAGE: Most dotted journals have this page only. Here you can use it for project brainstorming, novel plot planning, prompted writing sprints, notes from classes or seminars, trip reports, doodling, or coloring. You can use a blank page as a "container" of some projects: write down the topic and initial ideas; every time you have additional ideas, add a bullet list on that page. You can also create or explore your own templates with these pages.

COLORED PENS, STICKERS, and WASHI TAPES: Have fun with them. I use colored pens for decoration and for noting various status of a task (to continue, to wait for something else, etc.). I paste cute stickers for an artistic touch here and there. Washi tapes can brighten up a page easily.

Excerpts of Apple's Journal of November 2023 as Use Examples

Page	Subject
1	2023.11. Monthly tasks
3	2023.11. Monthly glance (BDs, VHP tasks)
5	2023.11. Daily trackers
7-12	2023.11. Wants - Gratitude - Affirmation
13	11.01.
15	11.02. An idea of publishing a BuJo notebook for myself.
17	11.03. Chatted w M.
19	11.04.
21	11.05.
23	11.06. May called from CA.
25	11.07.
27	11.08. 1st brainstorming of the children's book series. See P75. First snow, 3". A tease.
29	11.09.
31	11.10. FADS goodbye to Ivan and Valeria
33	11.11
35	11.12.
37	11.13.
39	11.14

Index

Page	Subject
75	Brainstorm children's picture series To be continued

2023.11

- NaNoWriMo for BK-M1 (finish it)
- All-in-One pub for New Year of 2024
- Anthology email list, call
- Children's books idea

- Fam gathering

- ECIS submit

2023.12

- BK-M1 revision; cover brainstorming
- All-in-One updates based on tests
- Anthology instr for submission
- Children's books test

- Fam gathering
- College tuition/bills for T & A
- Jury duty

- SC ready for sub; outlet
- APC reviews
- New LMS ready for Spring 2024

2024.01

- BK-M1 to editor; register; cover/title
- Anthology 1st sub due
- Children's: Book 1 design, research

- Vacation

- SC submit
- Prep teaching
- APC/Annual reviews
- GIS new search

Future log

2024.02

- BK-M1 revision, Beta reading

- Anthology title, register

- Children's book register, cover

2024.03

- BK-M1 revision, prep for launch

- All-in-One updates based on feedback

- ECIS result, revision

- GIS coding done

2024.04

BK-M1 launch

- Anthology final subs due, format, design, cover

- GIS analysis done

Future Log

November, 2023

Research
- ECIS submit
- SC draft
- MisInfo Proj Cont' Prep June conf

Teaching
- Prep finals
- Grade HW4
- Grade Q3
- Learn new LMS:
  Sign up demos
  Set up classes

Service
- Students recomm letters (4x10)
- APC for 2 colleagues
- Curriculum comm
- Program comm
- Fac meeting

Health
- 3rd month intermittent fasting monitor
- Annual physical
- Vertigo followup

Family/Friends
- Thanksgiving fam gathering
- Call family in China
- FADS party & bye to Ivan & Valeria
- Call Jen K

Garden/Chickens
- Plant spinach
- Cover mints w cardboards
- Clean coop (x2)

Monthly Goals

Writing
- NaNoWriMo for BK-M1 (finish it)
- Magnet for BK-M0

Marketing
- BK-M0 Kindle Select free promo
- CraveBooks promo
- eReaderGirls promo
- Website update
- Amazon Ads create

Anthology
- plan a series?
- setup email list
- send calls
- prep instruction for sub

New Projects
- All-in-One
  - Brainstorming
  - Design
  - Self testing
  - Revising
  - Ask 3 friends
  - Finalizing
  - Upload to KDP
  - Upload to IS
  - Sales page setup
- Children's pic book series
  - Brainstorm plan
  - Collaborator?

Entertainment
- Tribute to John Denver
- Movies (x2)

Books
- "Finding Me" by Viola Davis
- "Broken Horses" by Brandi Carlile
- "The measure of our Age" by M.T. Connolly

Business
- Tax status appl
- Paypal acct set up

Monthly Goals

2023.11

Sun	Mon	Tue	Wed
			1 KK BD (how old?)
5	6	7	8
12	13	14	15
19 BK-MO promo	20 C 30th BD BK-MO promo	21	22
26	27	28	29 BK-MO LP submit

Month at a Glance

2023.11

Thu	Fri	Sat	Note
2	3 EE 31st BD	4	
9	10	11 Ivan 29th BD	
16 BK-MO promo	17 ECIS due BK-MO promo	18	
23	24	25	
30 All-in-One submit			

Month at a Glance

2023.11

Day	Eggs	Weight	Tennis	Hiking	Dance	Gardening /Snow plow	Meditation	Mood	Physical	Mental
1	2						10	3	2	2
2	2					90	10	3	3	3
3	3						20	2	2	2
4	1		90		45		10	3	3	3
5	4			30			10	2	2	2
6	1						10	3	3	3
7	3						10	2	2	3
8	2					20	20	3	3	3
9	2			60			10	3	3	3
10	3				120		10	1	1	2
11	1		90				10	3	3	3
12	2		180				10	3	3	3
13	2							3	3	3
14	1							3	3	3
15	1							3	3	3
16										
17										
18										
19										
20										
21										
22										
23										
24										
25										
26										
27										
28										
29										
30										
31										

Three of them seem to influence each other.

Mental sharpness better than Oct

Monthly Trackers

2023.11

Intermittent Fasting Tracking

Day	NaNoWriMo # words	fast hrs	1st calories	1st meal	last meal		notes
1		16	10:00	11:00	7:00		Headache
2	2229	15	10:00		5:30		
3		17	10:30	11:00	8:00		heahache
4	1525	14	10:00		7:15		
5	1636	16	11:15		6:00		
6		16	10:00	10:30	6:00		
7	338	16	10:00	11:00	6:30		
8		15.5	10:00		7:00		
9	1410	15	10:00		6:30		
10		16	10:30		6:00		
11	1487	16	10:00		6:00		
12	876	16.5	10:30		6:30		
13							
14							
15							
16							
17							
18							
19							
20							
21							
22							
23							
24							
25							
26							
27							
28							
29							
30							
31							

Monthly Trackers

November, 2023

Gratitude

1	Grateful to have such engaging and eager to learn students in both of my classes. The best a professor can ask for.
2	Grateful for a lovely fall season: not cold, not snowy (yet), and plenty of sunshine. Allowing plenty of outdoor activities.
3	Greatful for the encouragement from other authors in the NaNoWriMo event.
4	Grateful my headache is not too bad and I can still function. Could be a lot worse.
5	Thankful to have health and other benefits covered generously by the university.
6	Grateful to have my spiritual sisters in my PO8 group to support and cheer for each other selflessly.
7	
8	
9	
10	I am reminded how lucky I am to be able to dance which brings me so much joy and confidence in controlling my body.
11	
12	Grateful for 3 hours of high intensity tennis mixer! Great players tonight. Not too crowded thus no stop playing.

Daily Quotes

13	
14	Grateful to have art talent at home! T is tremendous help in teaching me Photoshop.
15	Grateful to be selected as a finalist for two categories, Women's and Multicultural, at the 2023 IAN Book of the Year Award!
16	
17	
18	
19	
20	Continue to be grateful for being the best role of the world during the last 30 years!
21	Grateful the kids are able to come back for Thanksgiving. Hoping I can hold my own - no sickness please!
22	
23	I am thankful for all I have in my life.
24	
25	Grateful for the quiet and uninterrupted time I have to focus on some tasks that are delayed due to sickness.
26	grateful Atticus is so easy to use! What a difference in comparison with Word! Well worth the money. A keeper. Too bad no Chinese characters yet.
27	
28	
29	Grateful I can still hold Zoom class despite being sick and students showed up!
30	Thanks for the encouragement and motivation from other authors, I finished the stories as I planned. Now on revision!
31	

Daily Quotes

11/2 Thur

v Completed   ! Delegated
> Forwarded   x Removed
- In Progress

To Do
- [v] Grade team projects
- [v] Prep meeting for tomorrow BuJo
- [v] Set up and catch up BK-MO
- [v] Large Print ISBN appl
- [>] Investment
- [v] BK-MO magnet photos/images
- [ ]
- [ ]

Meeting / Time
- [v] Mia on tax status — 11:30am
- [v] PagePal — 8:30-10:30am
- [v] B'Ville Lib — 5:30-8:30pm

Jotting, Doodling, Scribbling

654 Project grading:
- T1: 93%
- T2: 93%
- T3: 90%
- T4: 95%
- T5: missing part
- T6: 93%
- T7: 95%
- T8: 93%

Wow, great job!

PagePal: 59876-50241=1635
B'Ville: 62105-59876=2229

BuJo setup:
- what a chore to do templates, again.
- Hmmmm. My own journal?
- Maybe even cheaper than buying
- Check on KDP, estimate.

YES! Should go for it!

With Mia:
- Need additional documents
- Starting today, 11/2
- Quarterly filing regardless sales
- Can file online (tutorial)
- Will send email reminder
- Only for NY State
- (Knowledge is power. I could have done it myself if I know where and how. BUT: learn to delegate!)

To do for those Chinese Books:
- Classify
- Take pictures for later use
- Read them! Might be so different from 50 years ago!

Daily Log

| 11/2 Thur | Weather | High 46 / Low 33 | Sunny ✓ Partial Sunny Cloudy | Rainy Snow |

Reflections, Ideas, Diary

- A busy day as usually. Feels good to be productive.

- Mimi is recovering well. It has only been a week or so but she is able to put weight on her injured foot. She is in such a great spirit. When I said "You are a tough cookie," she replied, "I have to." It makes me giggle every time I realize she is 96. Such a pleasant person to be around.

- NaNoWriMo can be tough! 50,000 words for the month means about 1,700 words per day. If one misses one day, then one has to make it up to produce 3,400 words! For those meeting/teaching days, I have no choice but to miss. For today, I only wrote 2,229 words. Already behind. But even those 2,229 words made me proud. I can see why this event is so popular. It is a test of capacity and discipline. I do have a goal of finishing all the stories of BK-M1 by the end of November. Will try my best.

- Need to be a good caregiver to those books I picked up from J yesterday. J was worried that I might damage them. What!? Did I ever damage anything? But I can understand. These books are hard to find these days. She got some of them from the piles of recycled papers at a remote recycling plant in Beijing!

- These books share similar ideas with those comic books in the U.S. I wonder where the original idea was from. Might be interesting to do some digging.

- The girls are still producing eggs. Much different than the same time last year. Might be the warm weather so far.

- A nice day. Spent some quality time in the garden. Not sure how many such days left for the year. Although I think snow might be helpful to kill some germs.

Daily Log

Children's Picture Series Brainstorming   2023.11.08

- Series vs. Single books?
    - Series has volume and can build on *can keep going and evolving*
    - Single can be too thin

    Can each be independent? That would be cool!

- Content: can easily think of a few
    #1: Bonded forever
    #2: The crazy twins
    #3: I say you do
    #4:
    #5:
    #6:
    #7:

    Mostly done in BK-M1. Need to rewrite for picture books

- Age range: 3-10?

- Characters: two better than one
    - Dynamics
    - More aspects/meanings

- Possible title(s):
    - "The Story about A & B"?
    - Inspired by "The Story about Ping"

    - 31 pages
    - 50 words/page
    - 1500~2000 words/book

75

If T, test during holiday break

To Dos:

广, 主, 占, 习

- Find an illustrator who can draw Chinese girls and like the stories
- Check market and other feasibility factors
- Re-write the stories
  -> should this be novels based on true stories/events? (can be elaborated and dramatized)

- Check with some teachers or parents for readership?
  - J is a teacher herself!
  - American teachers or parents?
  - Children's Librarians?

Ask S for some additional insight?

- Other considerations:
  - Colored: light colors, not full dense colors
  - Size: not too big? easy for young children?

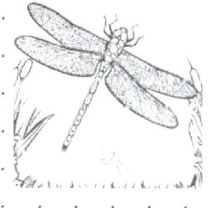

End of Use Examples for November 2023

Page	Subject

Index

Page	Subject

Page	Subject

Page	Subject

Future Log

Future Log

Monthly Goals

Monthly Goals

Sun	Mon	Tue	Wed

Month at a Glance

Thu	Fri	Sat	Note
☐	☐	☐	
☐	☐	☐	
☐	☐	☐	
☐	☐	☐	
☐	☐	☐	

Month at a Glance

1
2
3
4
5
6
7
8
9
10
11
12
13
14
15
16
17
18
19
20
21
22
23
24
25
26
27
28
29
30
31

Monthly Trackers

1
2
3
4
5
6
7
8
9
10
11
12
13
14
15
16
17
18
19
20
21
22
23
24
25
26
27
28
29
30
31

Monthly Trackers

1.
2.
3.
4.
5.
6.
7.
8.
9.
10.
11.
12.

Daily Quotes

13	
14	
15	
16	
17	
18	
19	
20	
21	
22	
23	
24	
25	
26	
27	
28	
29	
30	
31	

Daily Quotes

1.
2.
3.
4.
5.
6.
7.
8.
9.
10.
11.
12.

Daily Quotes

13	
14	
15	
16	
17	
18	
19	
20	
21	
22	
23	
24	
25	
26	
27	
28	
29	
30	
31	

Daily Quotes

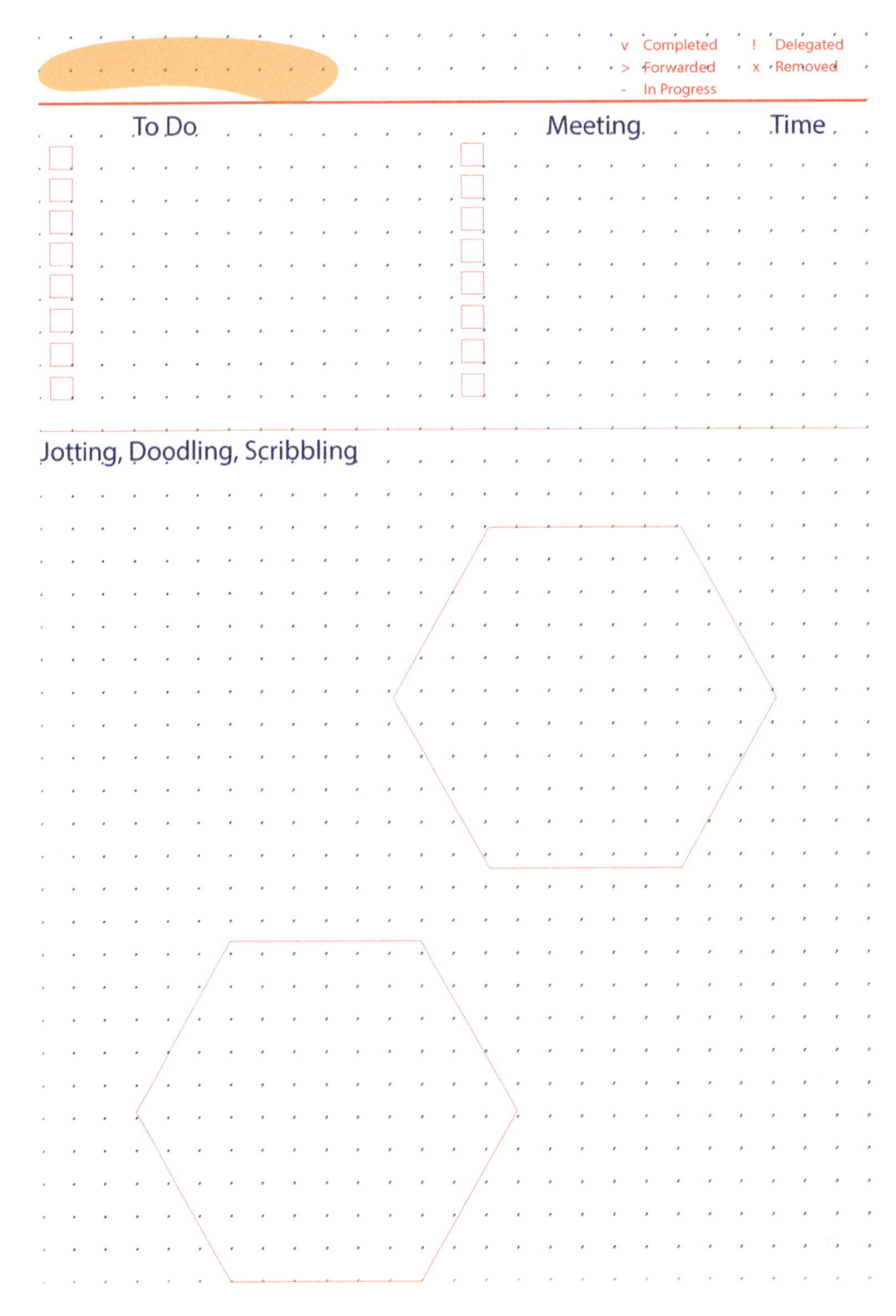

v Completed	! Delegated	
> Forwarded	x Removed	
- In Progress		

To Do

☐
☐
☐
☐
☐
☐
☐
☐
☐

Meeting

☐
☐
☐
☐
☐
☐
☐
☐

Time

Jotting, Doodling, Scribbling

Daily Log

Weather · High / Low · Sunny / Partial Sunny / Cloudy · Rainy / Snow

Reflections, Ideas, Diary

Daily Log

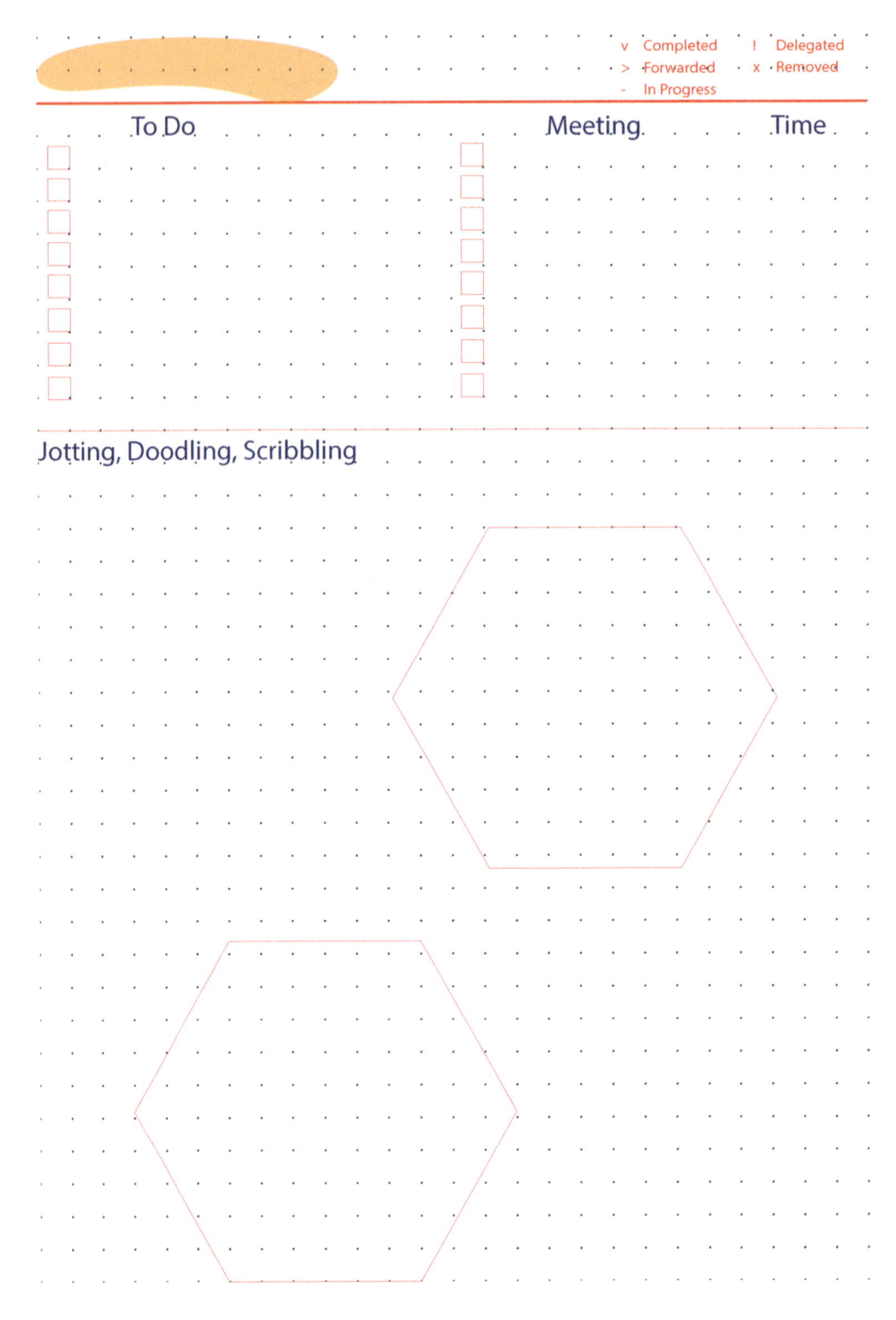

v Completed   ! Delegated
> Forwarded   x Removed
- In Progress

To Do   ## Meeting   ## Time

☐   ☐
☐   ☐
☐   ☐
☐   ☐
☐   ☐
☐   ☐
☐   ☐
☐   ☐

Jotting, Doodling, Scribbling

Daily Log

Weather · High / Low · Sunny · Partial Sunny · Cloudy · Rainy · Snow

Reflections, Ideas, Diary

Daily Log

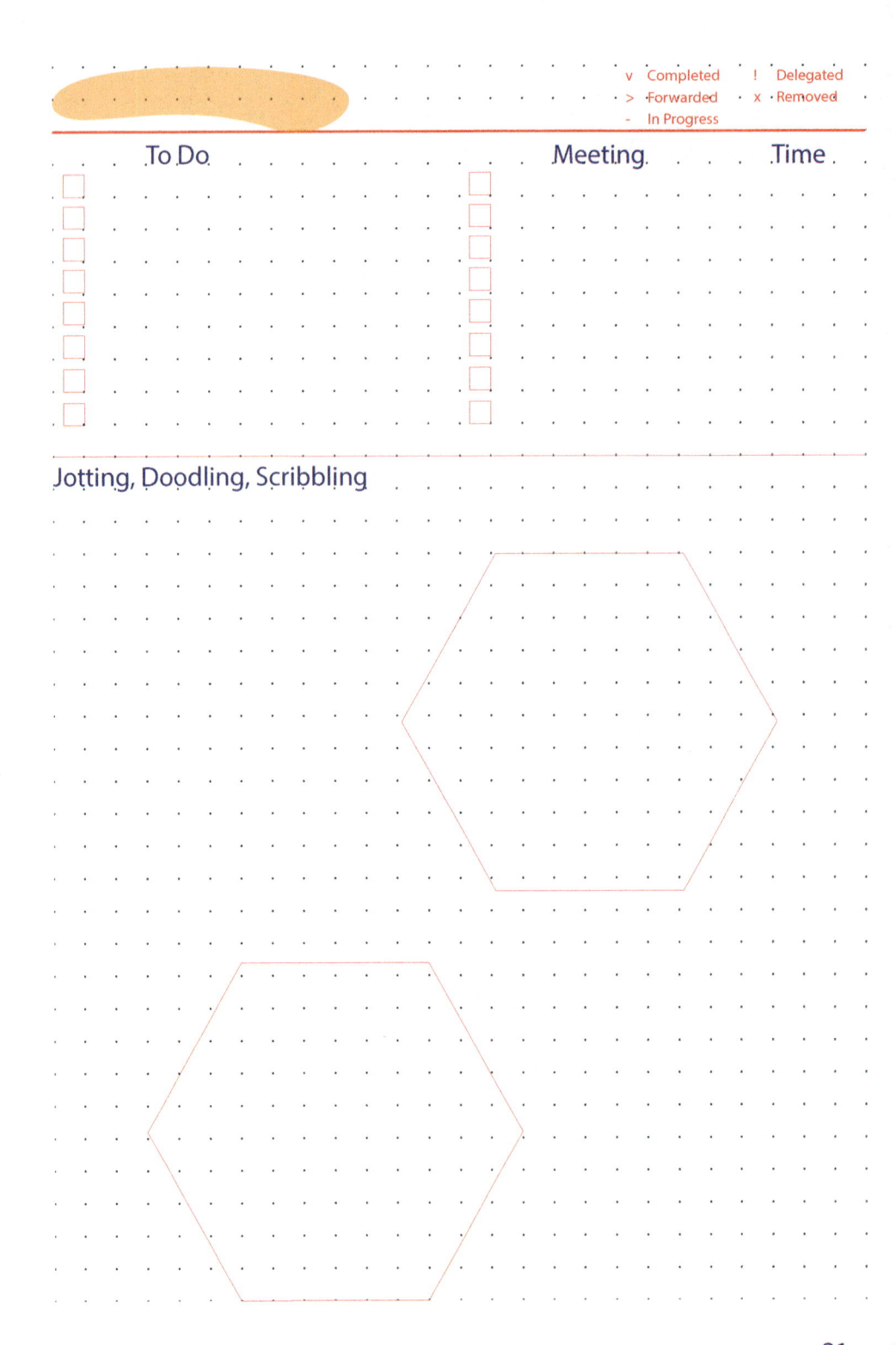

v Completed   ! Delegated
> Forwarded   x Removed
- In Progress

To Do   Meeting   Time

☐   ☐
☐   ☐
☐   ☐
☐   ☐
☐   ☐
☐   ☐
☐   ☐
☐   ☐

Jotting, Doodling, Scribbling

Daily Log

| Weather | High / Low | Sunny / Partial Sunny / Cloudy | Rainy / Snow |

Reflections, Ideas, Diary

	v	Completed	!	Delegated
	>	Forwarded	x	Removed
	-	In Progress		

To Do   Meeting   Time

☐
☐   ☐
☐   ☐
☐   ☐
☐   ☐
☐   ☐
☐   ☐
☐   ☐
☐   ☐

Jotting, Doodling, Scribbling

Daily Log   23

Weather   High   Sunny   Rainy
           Low   Partial Sunny Snow
                   Cloudy

Reflections, Ideas, Diary

Daily Log

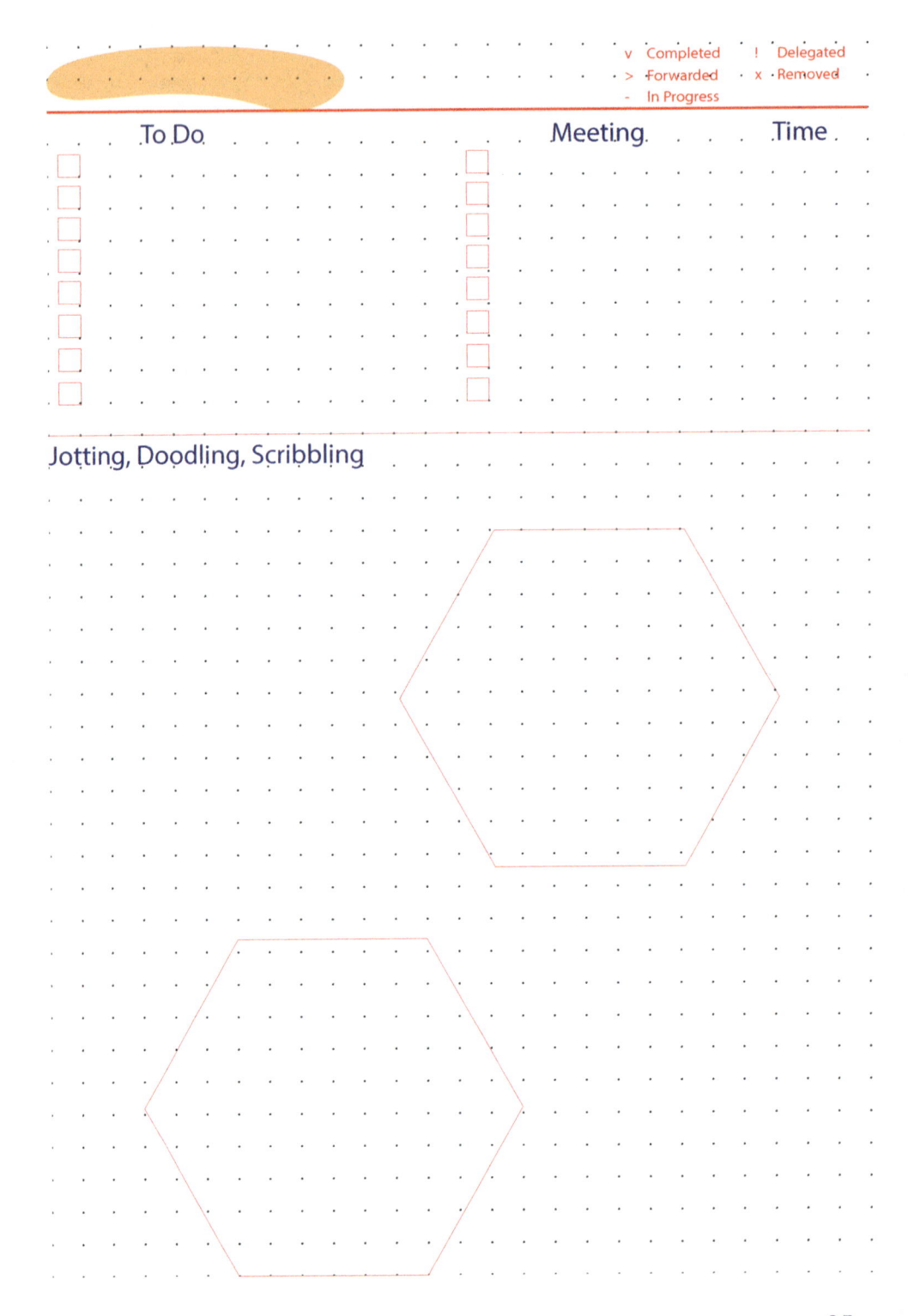

v Completed	! Delegated
> Forwarded	x Removed
- In Progress	

To Do

☐
☐
☐
☐
☐
☐
☐
☐
☐
☐

Meeting

☐
☐
☐
☐
☐
☐
☐
☐

Time

Jotting, Doodling, Scribbling

Daily Log

25

Weather   High   Sunny   Rainy
          Low   Partial Sunny   Snow
                 Cloudy

Reflections, Ideas, Diary

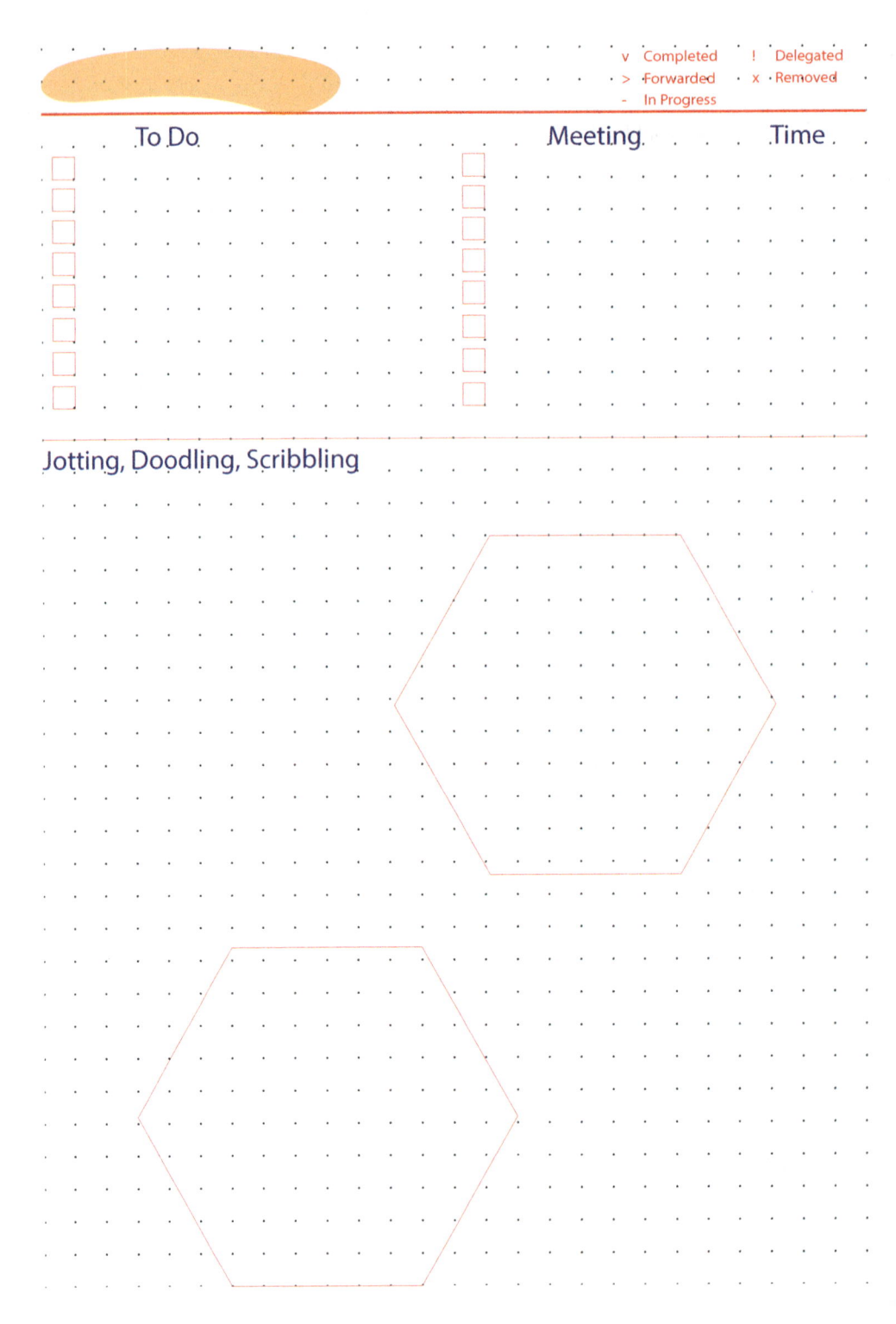

v Completed   ! Delegated
> Forwarded   x Removed
- In Progress

To Do   Meeting   Time

☐
☐
☐
☐
☐
☐
☐
☐
☐
☐

Jotting, Doodling, Scribbling

Daily Log

Weather · High · Sunny · Rainy
· Low · Partial Sunny · Snow
· Cloudy

Reflections, Ideas, Diary

Daily Log

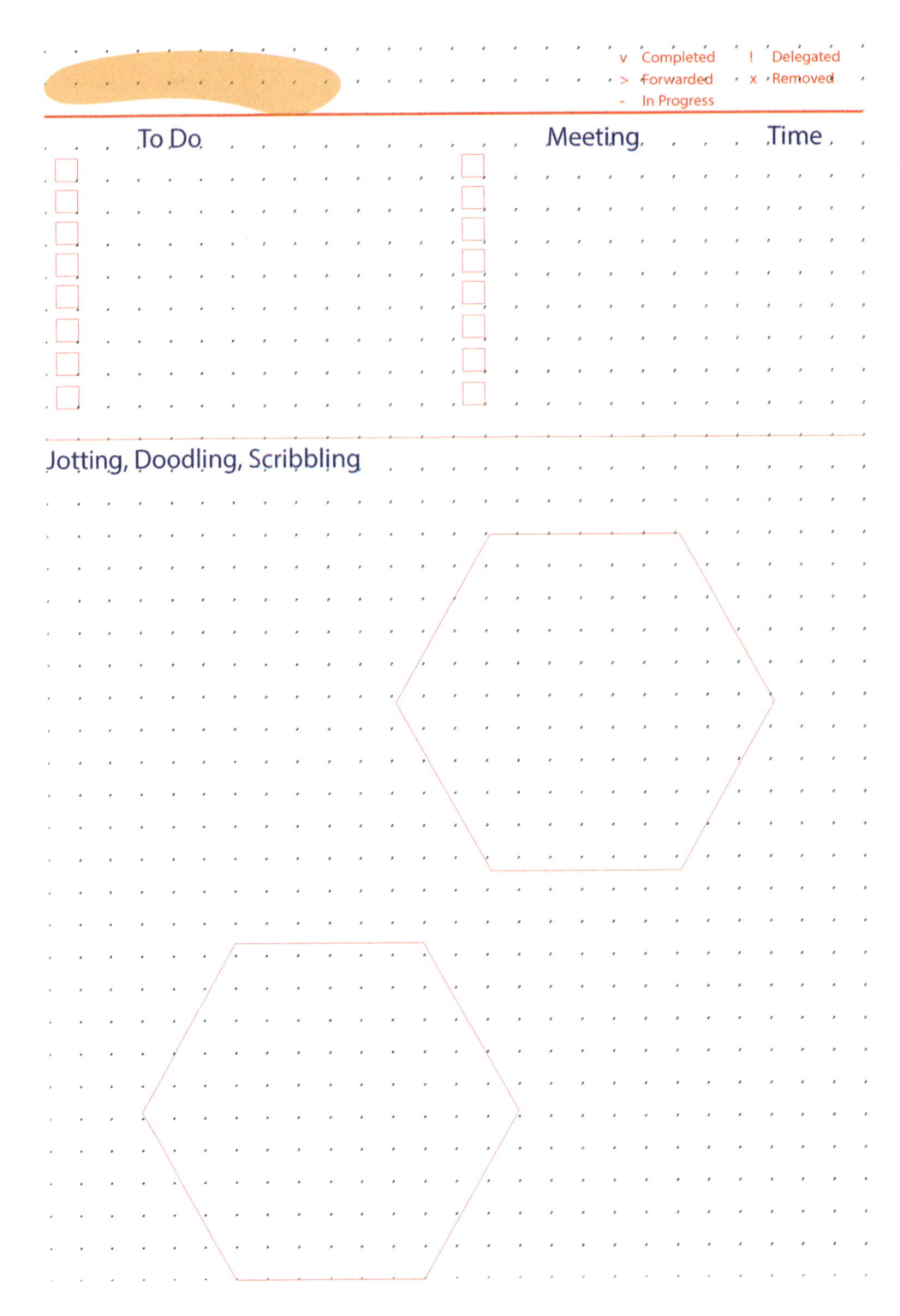

v	Completed	!	Delegated
>	Forwarded	x	Removed
-	In Progress		

To Do

☐
☐
☐
☐
☐
☐
☐
☐
☐
☐

Meeting   Time

☐
☐
☐
☐
☐
☐
☐

Jotting, Doodling, Scribbling

Weather   High   Sunny   Rainy
          Low   Partial Sunny Snow
                 Cloudy

Reflections, Ideas, Diary

Daily Log

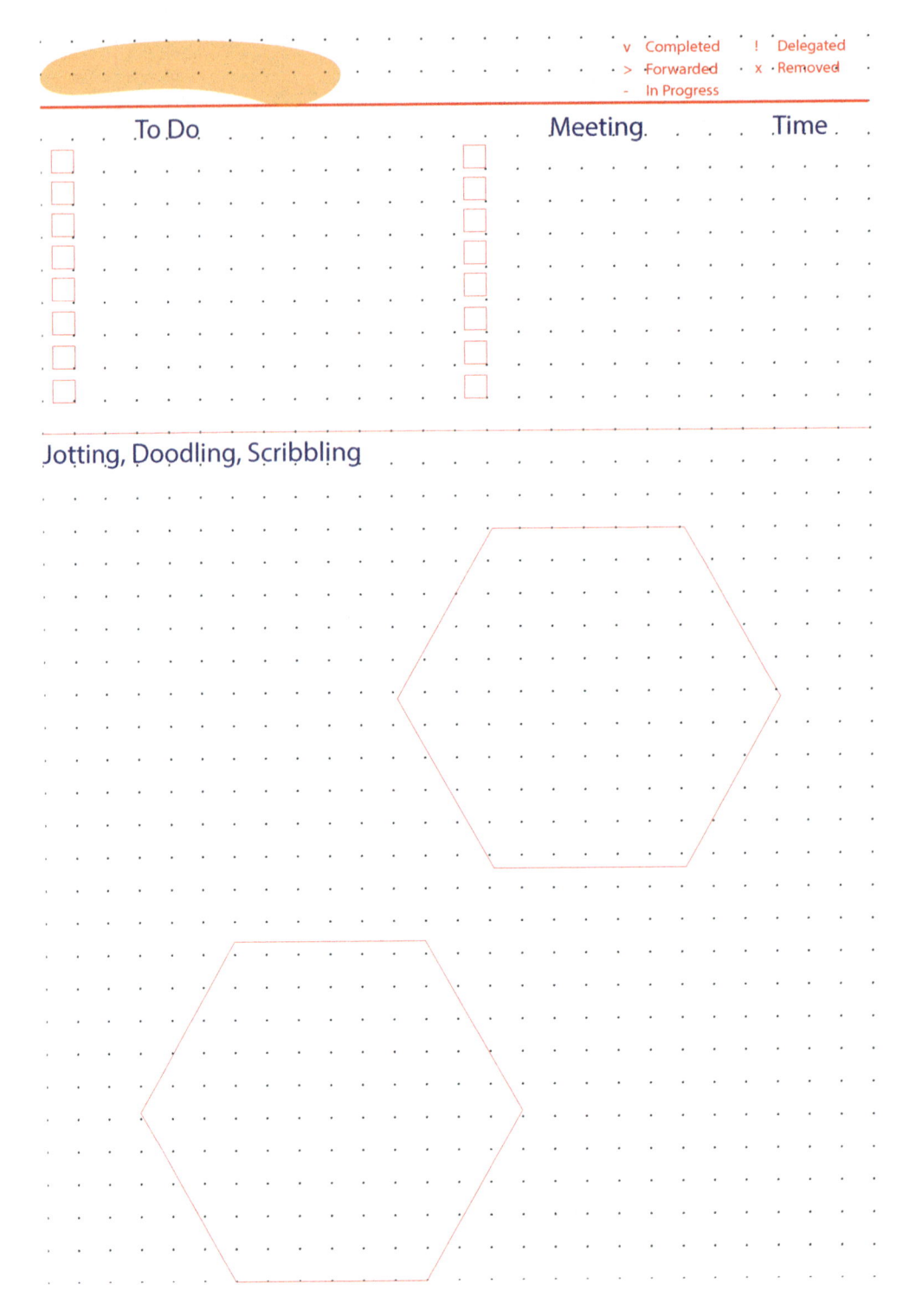

v Completed	! Delegated
> Forwarded	x Removed
- In Progress	

To Do · · · · · · · Meeting · · · Time

☐
☐
☐
☐
☐
☐
☐
☐

☐
☐
☐
☐
☐
☐
☐
☐

Jotting, Doodling, Scribbling

Daily Log   31

	Weather	High		Sunny	Rainy
		Low		Partial Sunny	Snow
				Cloudy	

Reflections, Ideas, Diary

v Completed	! Delegated
> Forwarded	x Removed
- In Progress	

To Do

Meeting

Time

Jotting, Doodling, Scribbling

Daily Log

Weather	High		Sunny	Rainy
	Low		Partial Sunny	Snow
			Cloudy	

Reflections, Ideas, Diary

Daily Log

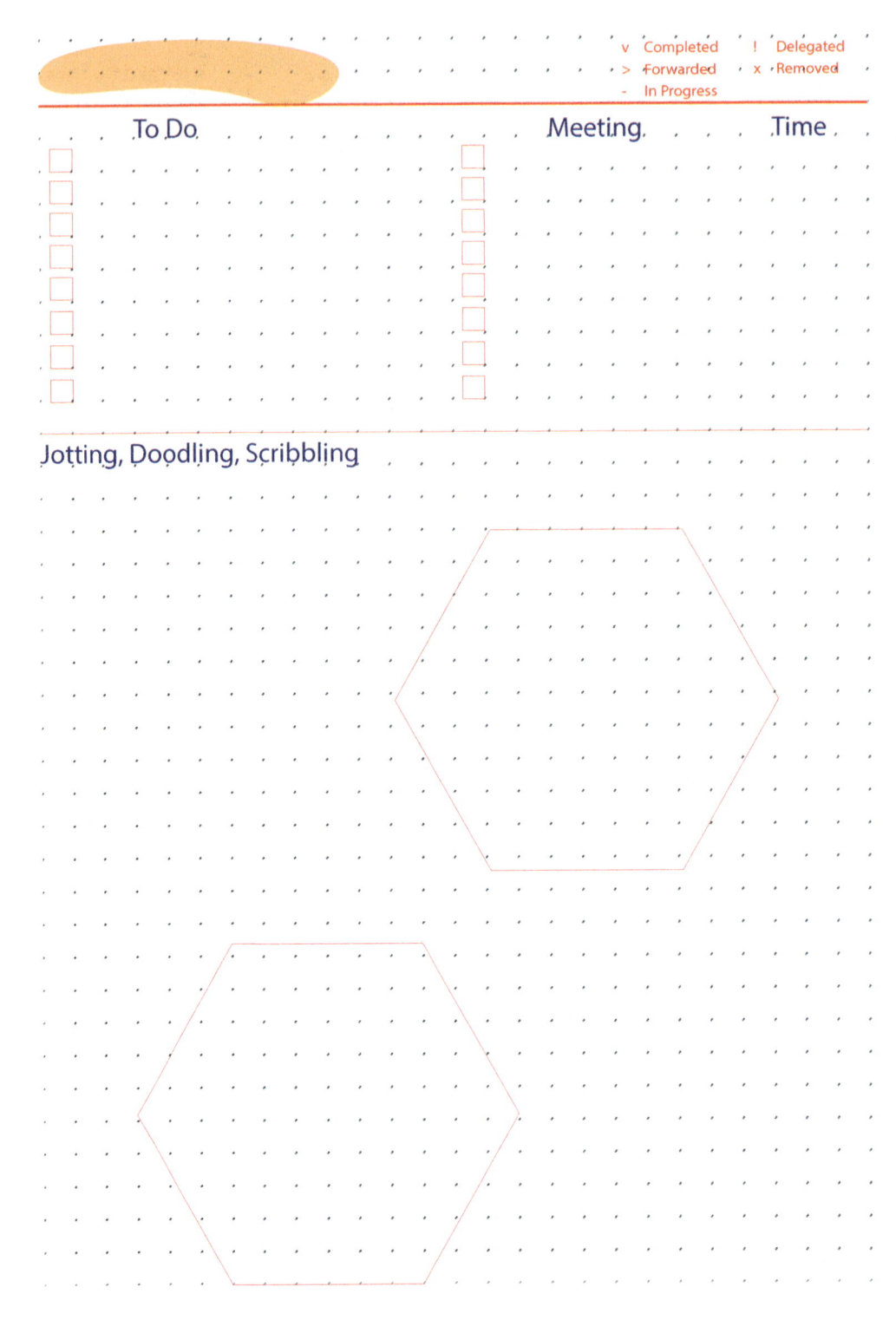

	v	Completed	!	Delegated
	>	Forwarded	x	Removed
	-	In Progress		

To Do

☐
☐
☐
☐
☐
☐
☐
☐
☐

Meeting

☐
☐
☐
☐
☐
☐
☐
☐
☐

Time

Jotting, Doodling, Scribbling

Daily Log

Weather | High | Sunny | Rainy
Low | Partial Sunny | Snow
Cloudy

Reflections, Ideas, Diary

Daily Log

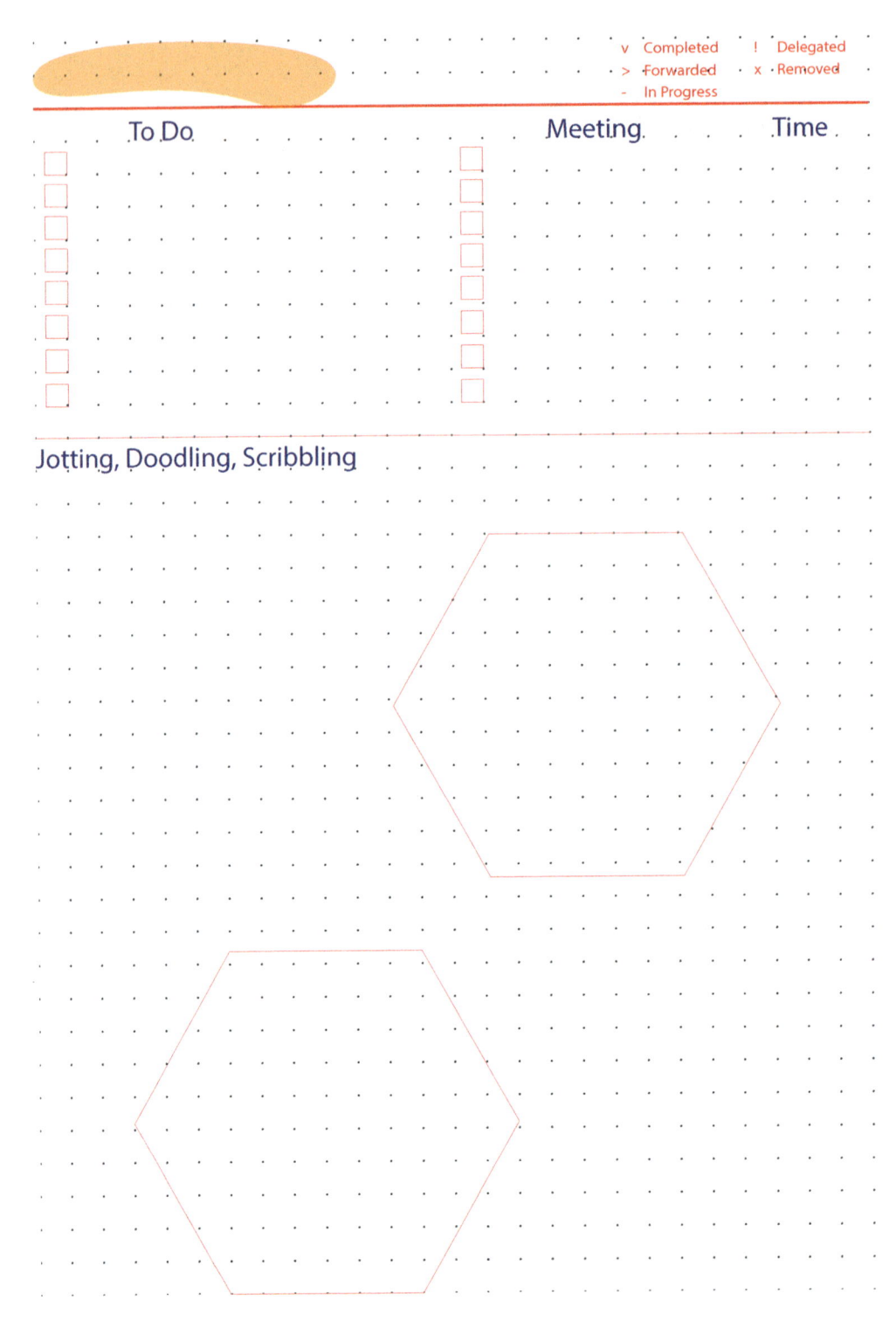

v Completed	! Delegated
> Forwarded	x Removed
- In Progress	

To Do   ## Meeting   ## Time

☐
☐
☐
☐
☐
☐
☐
☐
☐

☐
☐
☐
☐
☐
☐
☐
☐
☐

Jotting, Doodling, Scribbling

Daily Log

Weather · High / Low · Sunny · Partial Sunny · Cloudy · Rainy · Snow

Reflections, Ideas, Diary

v Completed   ! Delegated
> Forwarded   x Removed
- In Progress

To Do

- [ ]
- [ ]
- [ ]
- [ ]
- [ ]
- [ ]
- [ ]
- [ ]
- [ ]
- [ ]

Meeting   Time

- [ ]
- [ ]
- [ ]
- [ ]
- [ ]
- [ ]
- [ ]
- [ ]

Jotting, Doodling, Scribbling

Daily Log

Weather | High | Sunny | Rainy
Low | Partial Sunny | Snow
Cloudy

Reflections, Ideas, Diary

v Completed   ! Delegated
> Forwarded   x Removed
- In Progress

To Do   Meeting   Time

☐
☐
☐
☐
☐
☐
☐
☐
☐

☐
☐
☐
☐
☐
☐
☐

Jotting, Doodling, Scribbling

Daily Log

Weather　High　　Sunny　　　　Rainy
　　　　　Low　　Partial Sunny　Snow
　　　　　　　　　Cloudy

Reflections, Ideas, Diary

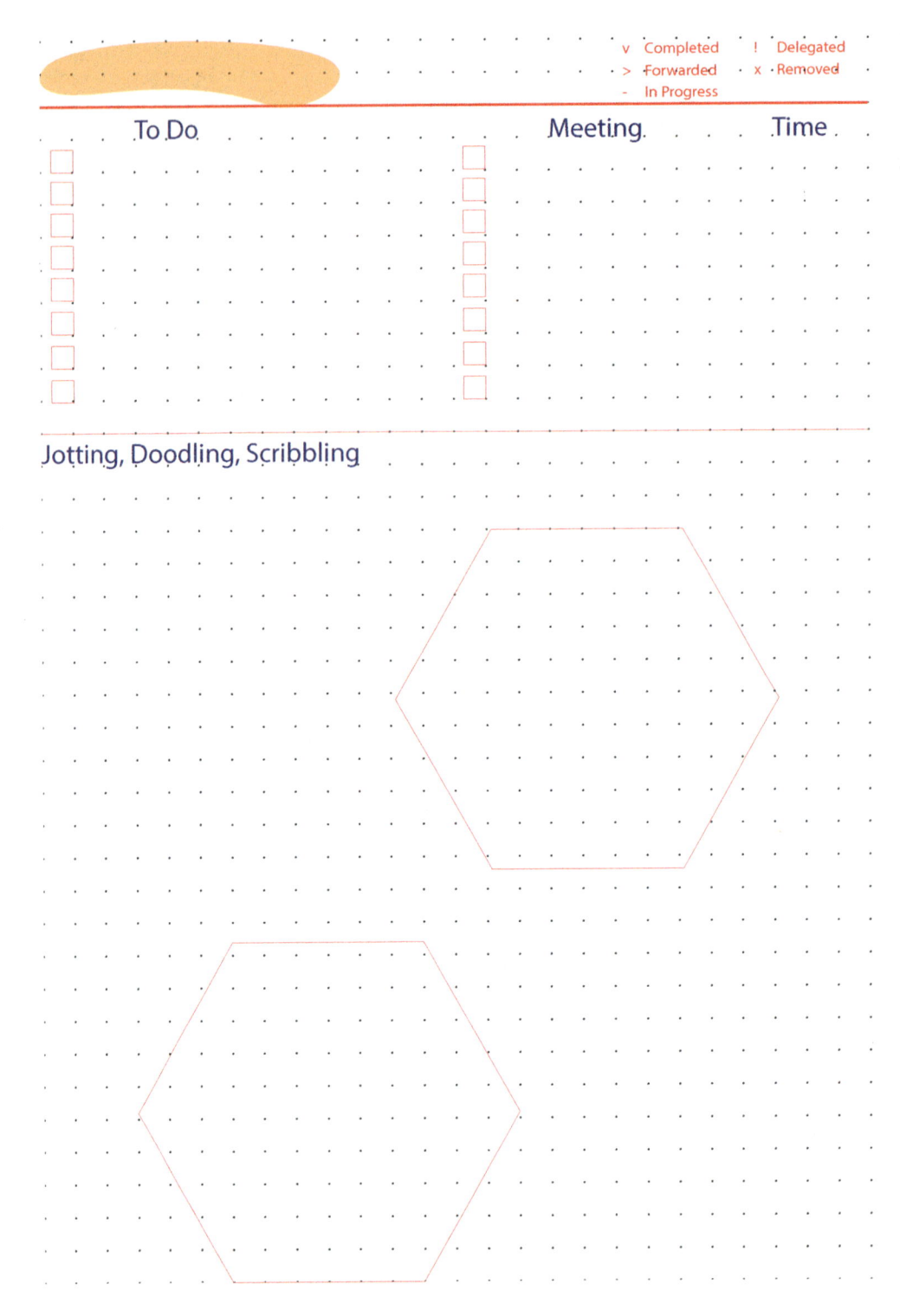

	v Completed	! Delegated
	> Forwarded	x Removed
	- In Progress	

To Do   Meeting   Time

Jotting, Doodling, Scribbling

Weather · High / Low · Sunny · Partial Sunny · Cloudy · Rainy · Snow

Reflections, Ideas, Diary

Daily Log 44

v	Completed	!	Delegated
>	Forwarded	x	Removed
-	In Progress		

To Do   Meeting   Time

☐
☐
☐   ☐
☐   ☐
☐   ☐
☐   ☐
☐   ☐
☐   ☐
☐   ☐
☐

Jotting, Doodling, Scribbling

Daily Log

Weather	High		Sunny	Rainy
	Low		Partial Sunny	Snow
			Cloudy	

Reflections, Ideas, Diary

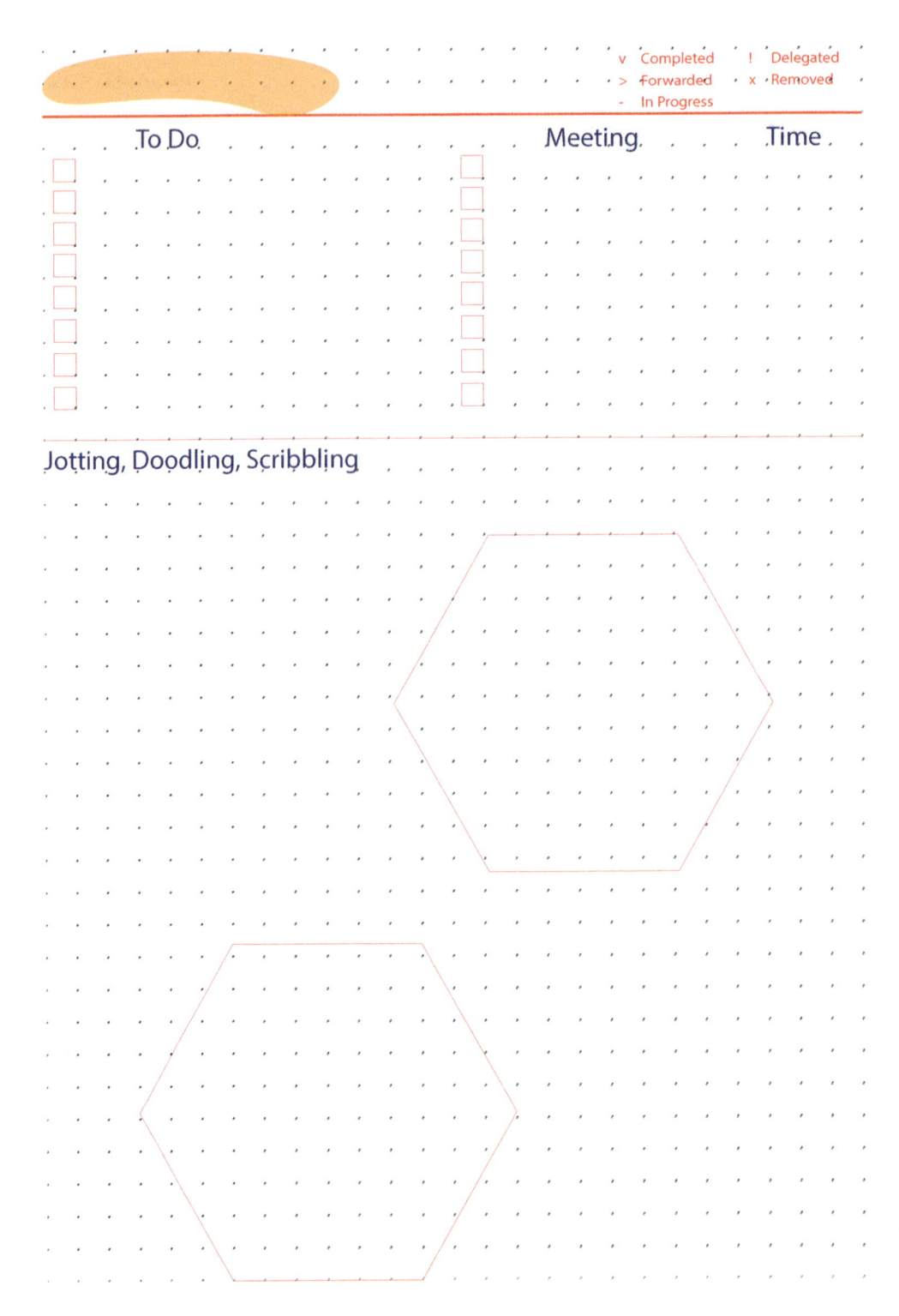

v Completed ! Delegated
> Forwarded x Removed
- In Progress

To Do

☐
☐
☐
☐
☐
☐
☐
☐
☐

Meeting   Time

☐
☐
☐
☐
☐
☐
☐
☐

Jotting, Doodling, Scribbling

Daily Log

Weather	High		Sunny	Rainy
	Low		Partial Sunny	Snow
			Cloudy	

Reflections, Ideas, Diary

Daily Log

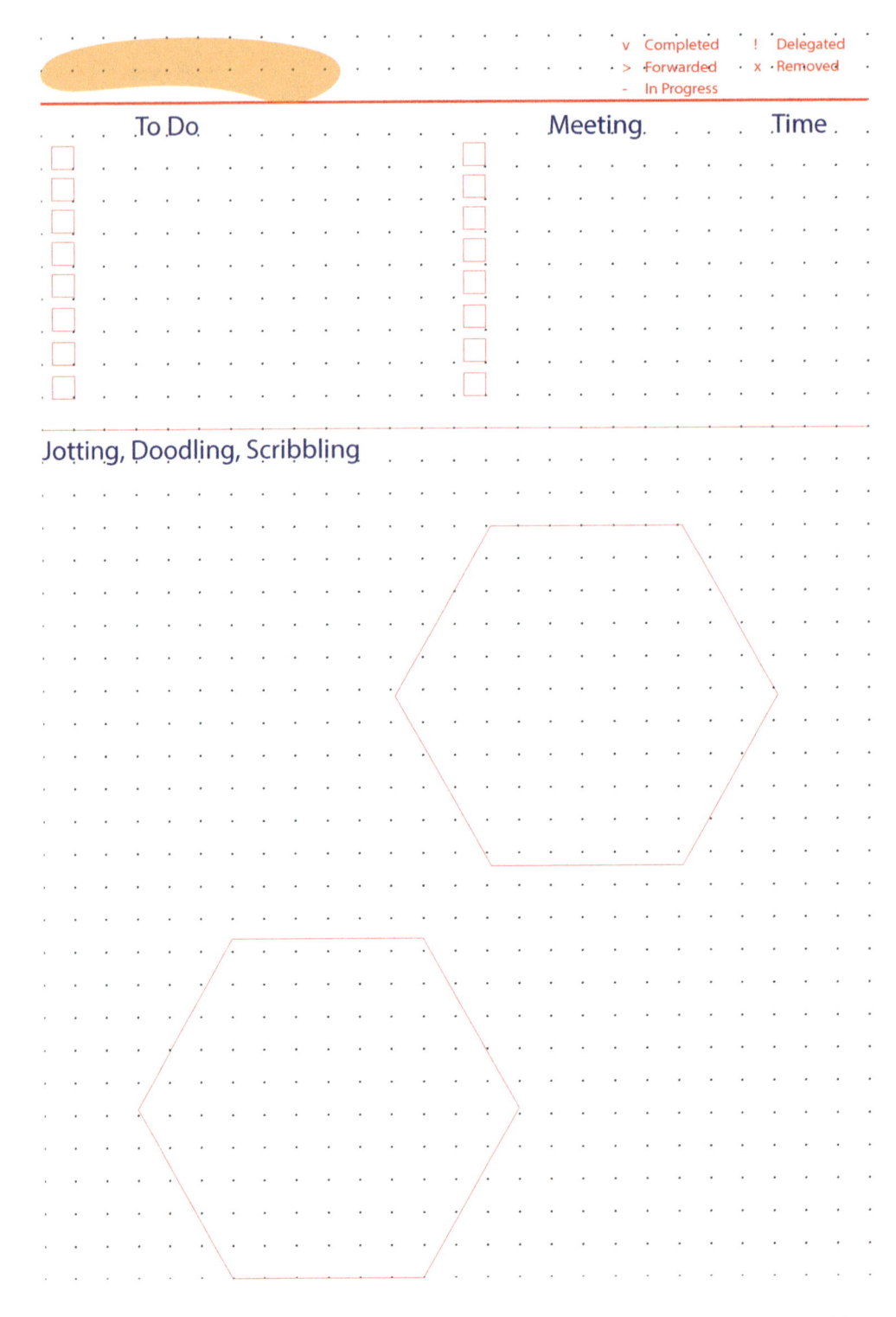

v Completed   ! Delegated
> Forwarded   x Removed
- In Progress

To Do

☐
☐
☐
☐
☐
☐
☐
☐
☐
☐

Meeting

☐
☐
☐
☐
☐
☐
☐
☐

Time

Jotting, Doodling, Scribbling

Daily Log

Weather | High / Low | Sunny / Partial Sunny / Cloudy | Rainy / Snow

Reflections, Ideas, Diary

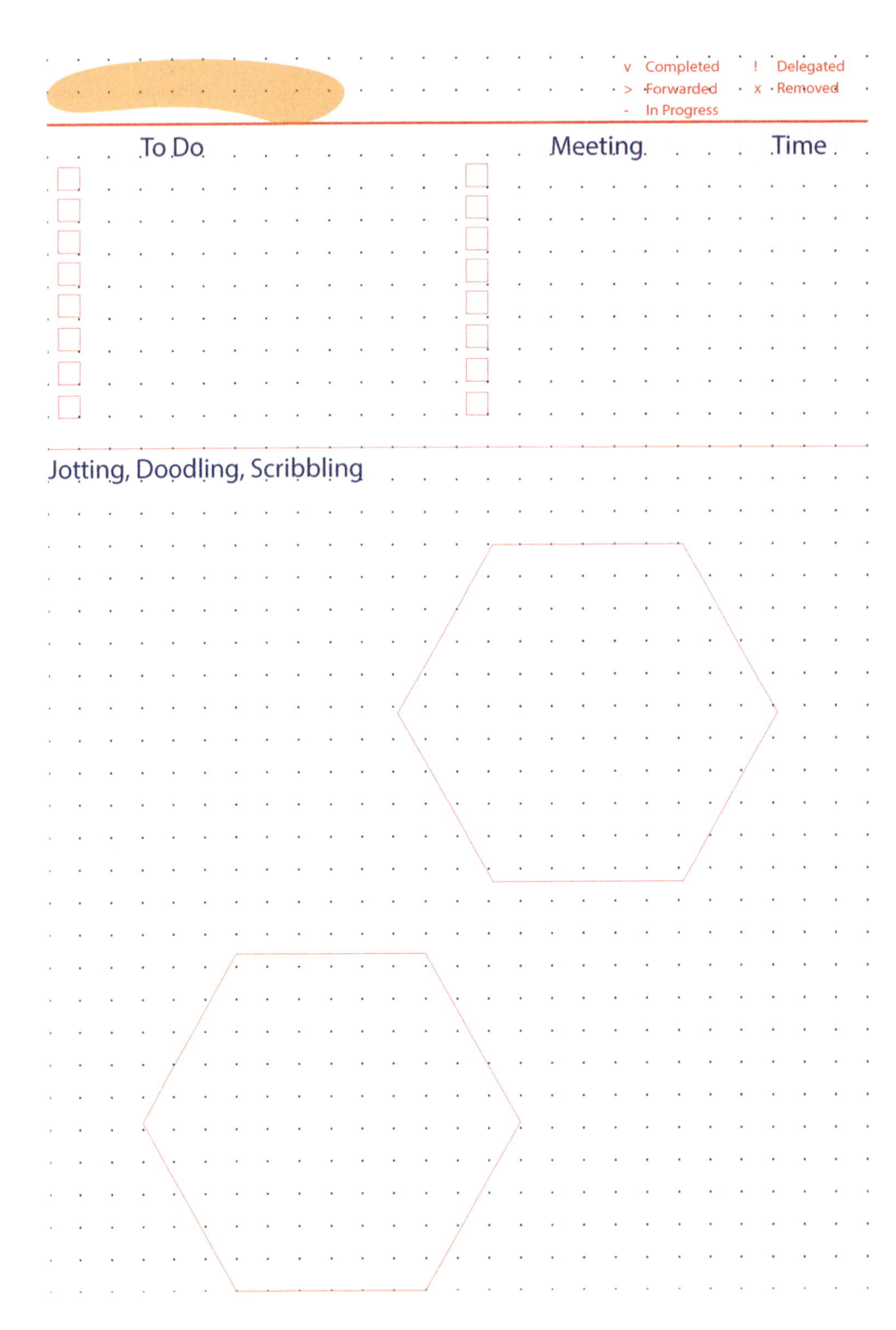

	v	Completed	!	Delegated
	>	Forwarded	x	Removed
	-	In Progress		

To Do   Meeting   Time

☐
☐
☐   ☐
☐   ☐
☐   ☐
☐   ☐
☐   ☐
☐   ☐
☐   ☐
☐   ☐

Jotting, Doodling, Scribbling

Daily Log

Weather   High   Sunny   Rainy
          Low   Partial Sunny Snow
                 Cloudy

Reflections, Ideas, Diary

Daily Log

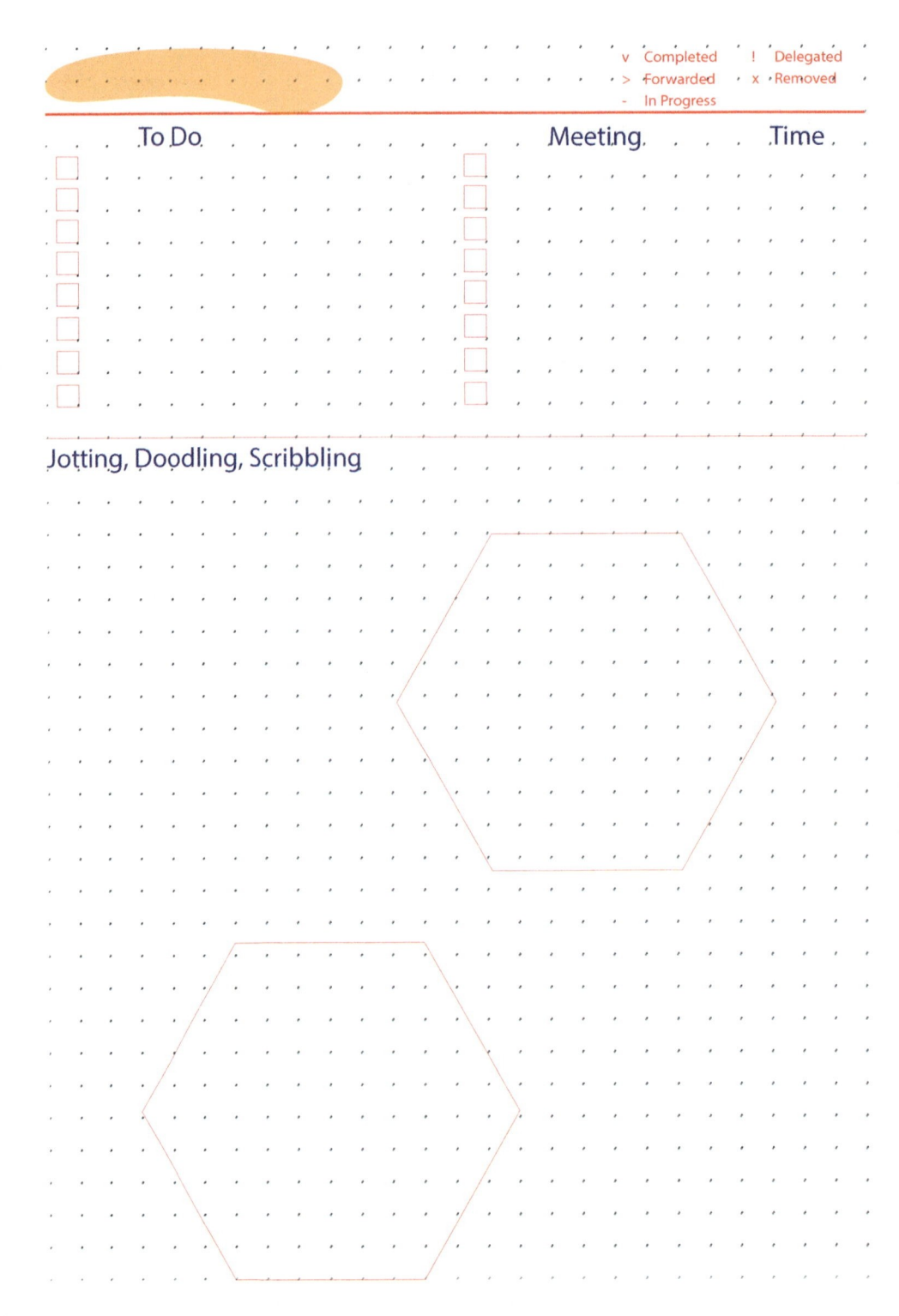

	v	Completed	!	Delegated
	>	Forwarded	x	Removed
	-	In Progress		

To Do

☐
☐
☐
☐
☐
☐
☐
☐
☐

Meeting Time

☐
☐
☐
☐
☐
☐
☐
☐

Jotting, Doodling, Scribbling

Daily Log

| Weather | High Low | | Sunny Partial Sunny Cloudy | Rainy Snow |

Reflections, Ideas, Diary

Daily Log 54

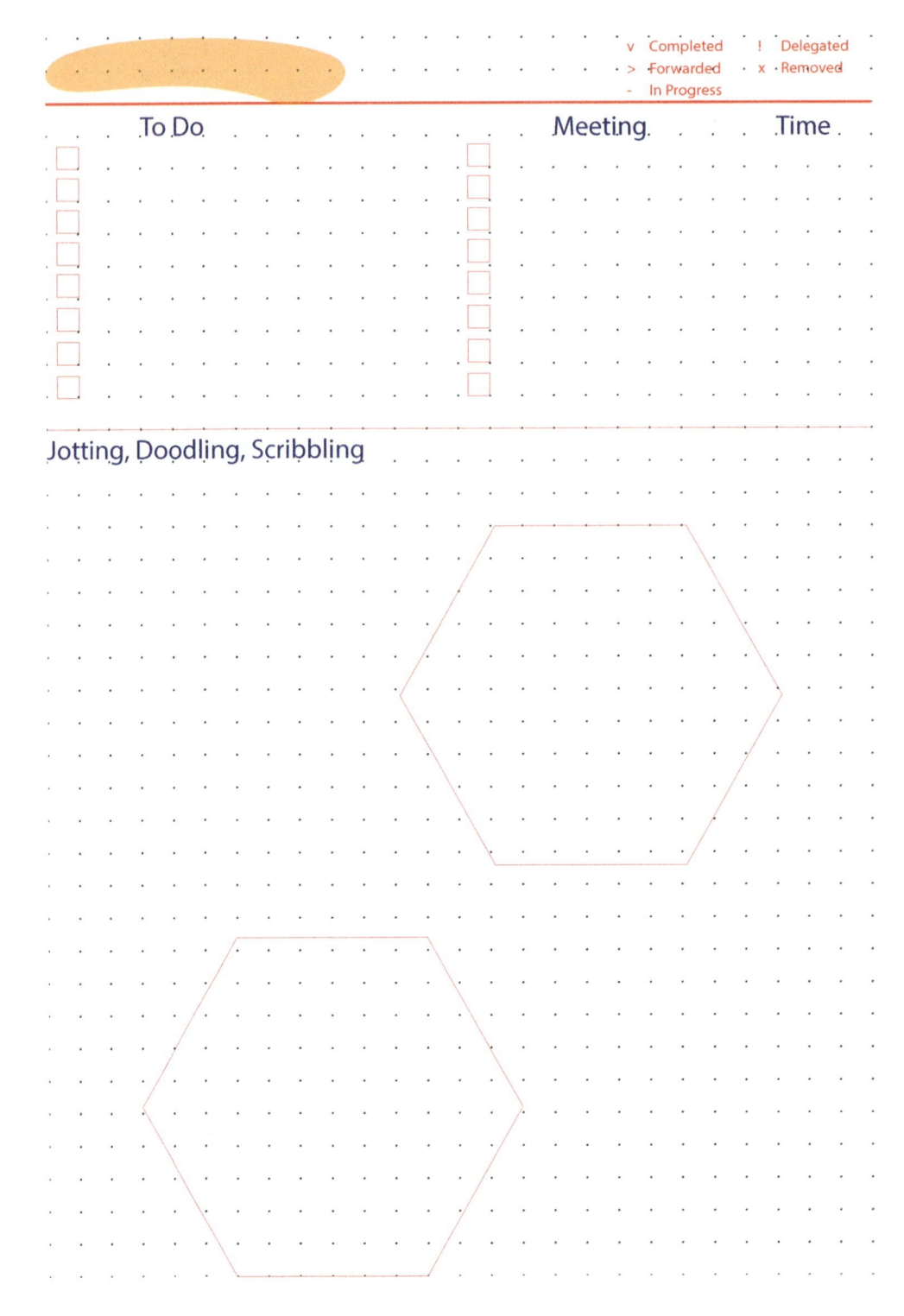

v Completed	! Delegated
> Forwarded	x Removed
- In Progress	

To Do

☐
☐
☐
☐
☐
☐
☐
☐
☐

Meeting   Time

☐
☐
☐
☐
☐
☐
☐
☐
☐

Jotting, Doodling, Scribbling

Daily Log

	Weather	High		Sunny	Rainy
		Low		Partial Sunny	Snow
				Cloudy	

Reflections, Ideas, Diary

Daily Log

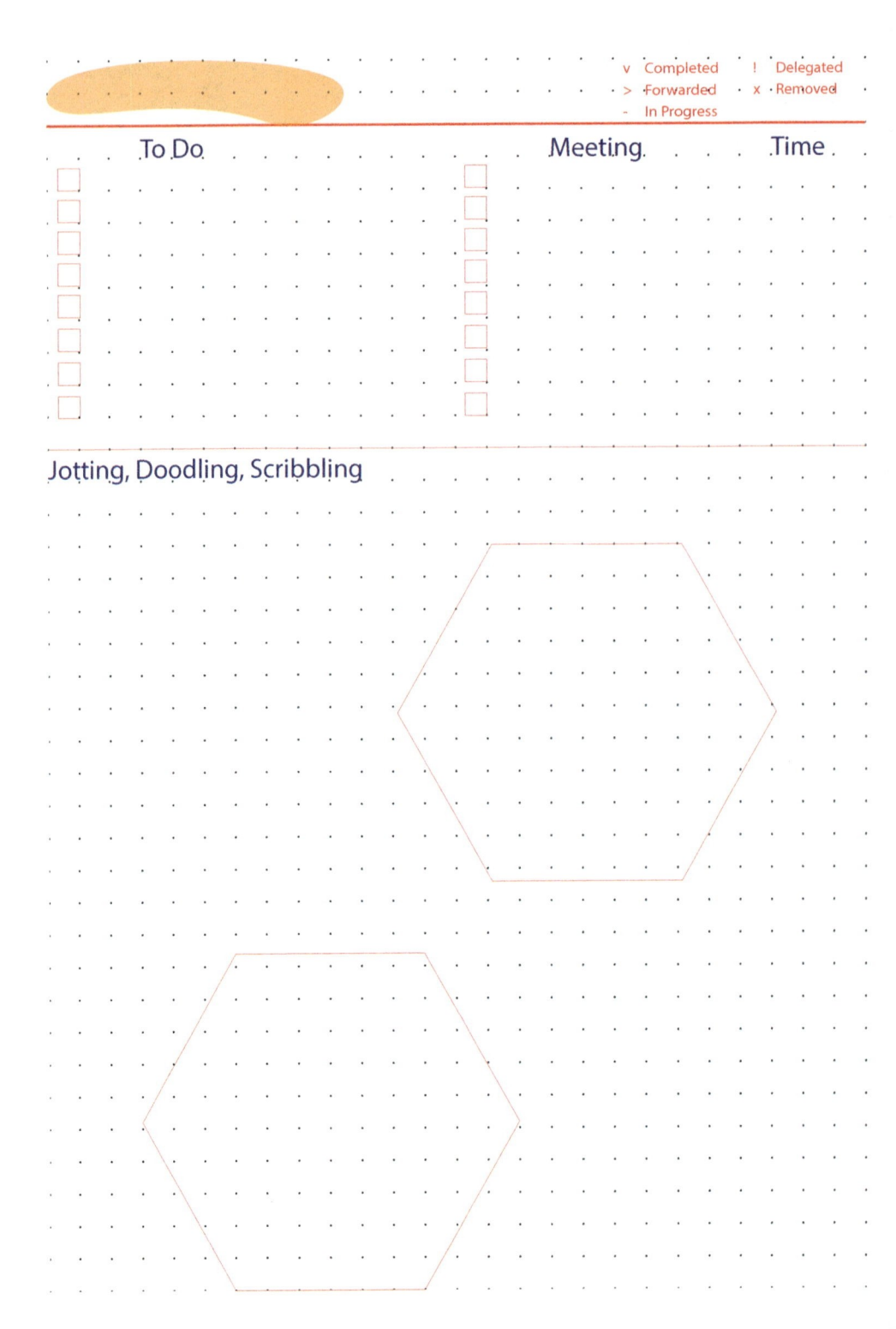

v Completed   ! Delegated
> Forwarded   x Removed
- In Progress

To Do   Meeting   Time

Jotting, Doodling, Scribbling

Daily Log

Weather · High / Low · Sunny · Partial Sunny · Cloudy · Rainy · Snow

Reflections, Ideas, Diary

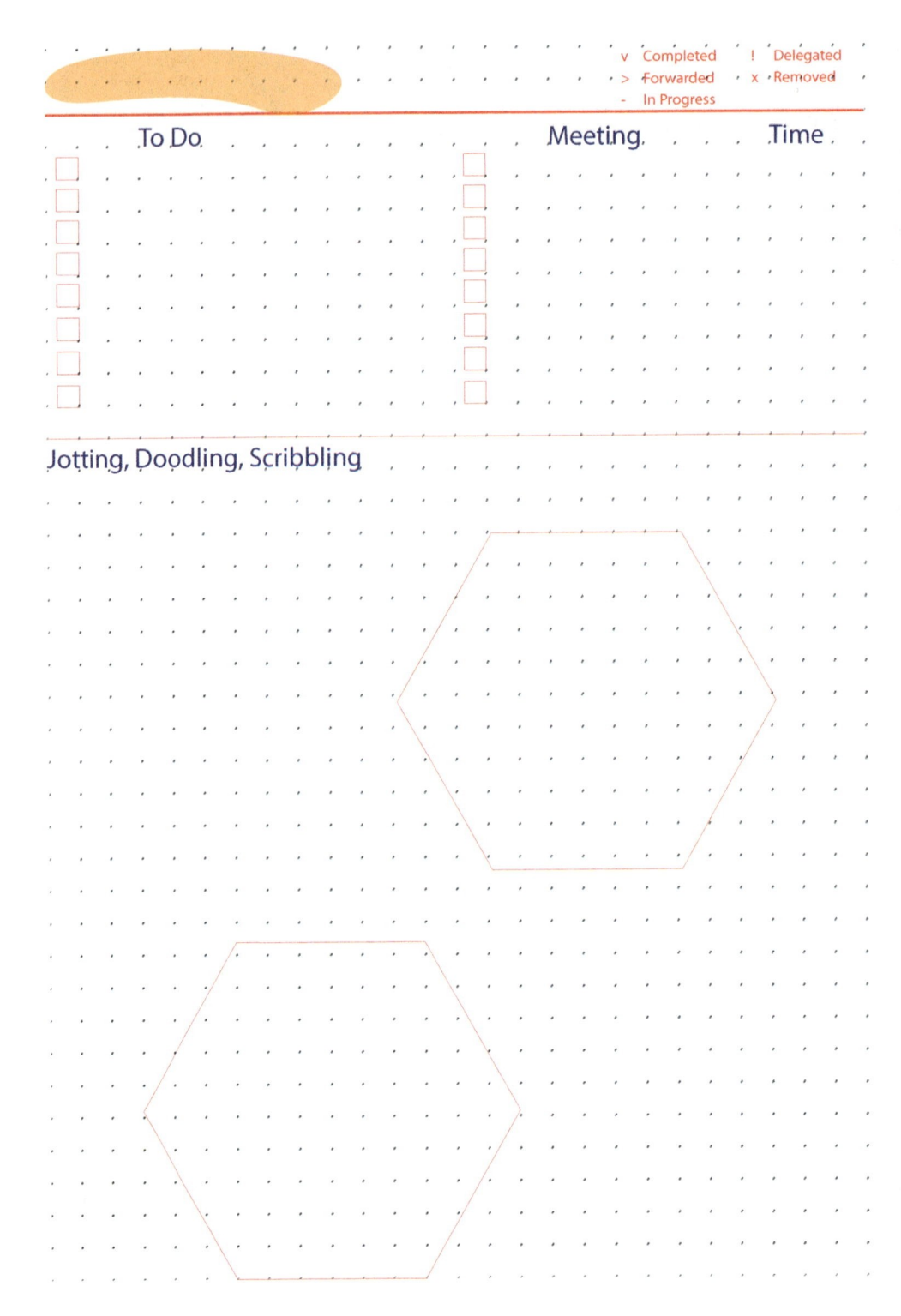

v Completed	! Delegated	
> Forwarded	x Removed	
- In Progress		

To Do

- [ ]
- [ ]
- [ ]
- [ ]
- [ ]
- [ ]
- [ ]
- [ ]
- [ ]

Meeting / Time

- [ ]
- [ ]
- [ ]
- [ ]
- [ ]
- [ ]
- [ ]
- [ ]

Jotting, Doodling, Scribbling

Daily Log

Weather	High	Sunny	Rainy
	Low	Partial Sunny	Snow
		Cloudy	

Reflections, Ideas, Diary

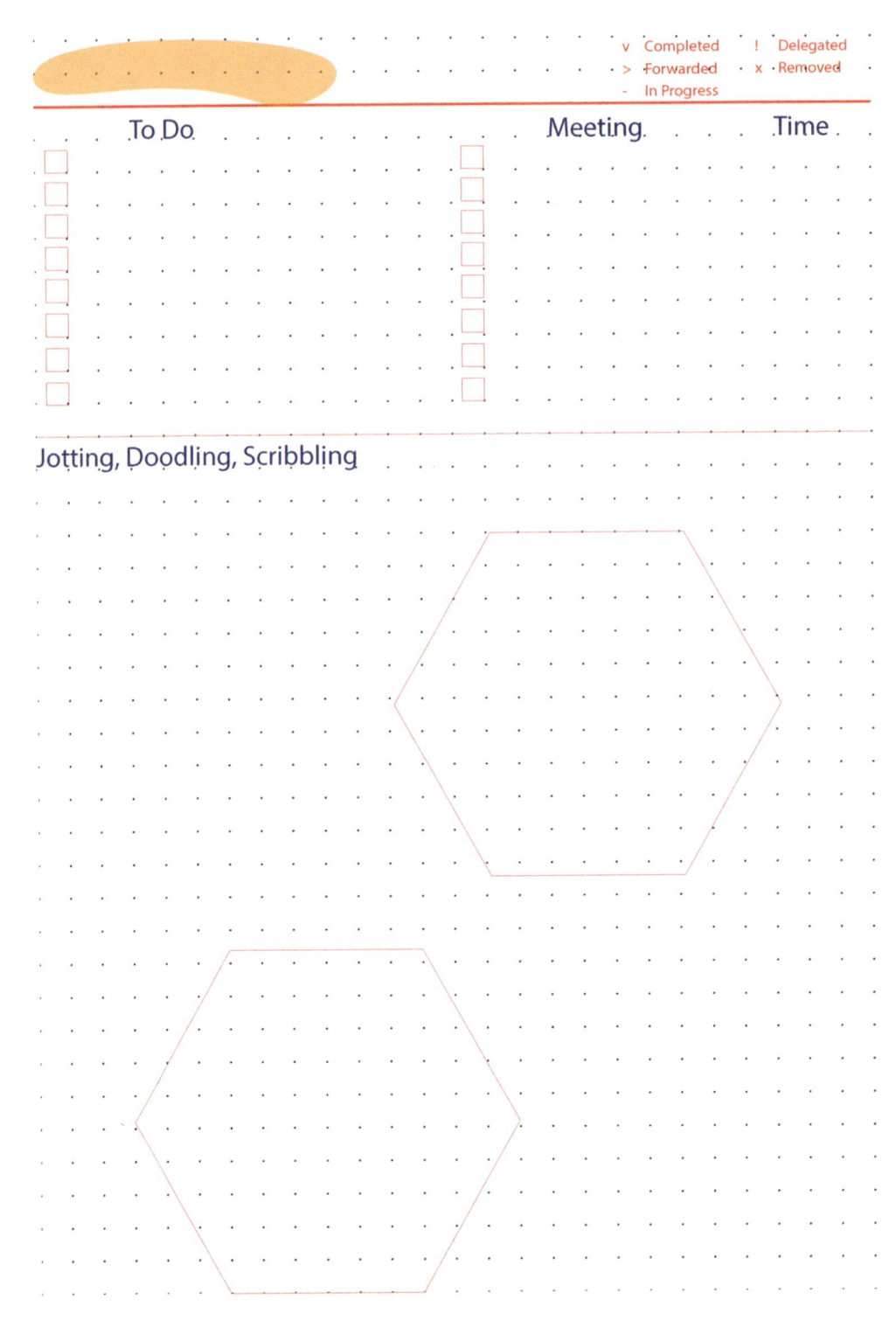

v Completed	! Delegated
> Forwarded	x Removed
- In Progress	

To Do

☐
☐
☐
☐
☐
☐
☐
☐

Meeting

☐
☐
☐
☐
☐
☐
☐
☐

Time

Jotting, Doodling, Scribbling

Daily Log

Weather · High / Low · Sunny / Partial Sunny / Cloudy · Rainy / Snow

Reflections, Ideas, Diary

v Completed   ! Delegated
> Forwarded   x Removed
- In Progress

To Do   ### Meeting   ### Time

☐   ☐
☐   ☐
☐   ☐
☐   ☐
☐   ☐
☐   ☐
☐   ☐
☐   ☐
☐

Jotting, Doodling, Scribbling

Daily Log

Weather · High / Low · Sunny / Partial Sunny / Cloudy · Rainy / Snow

Reflections, Ideas, Diary

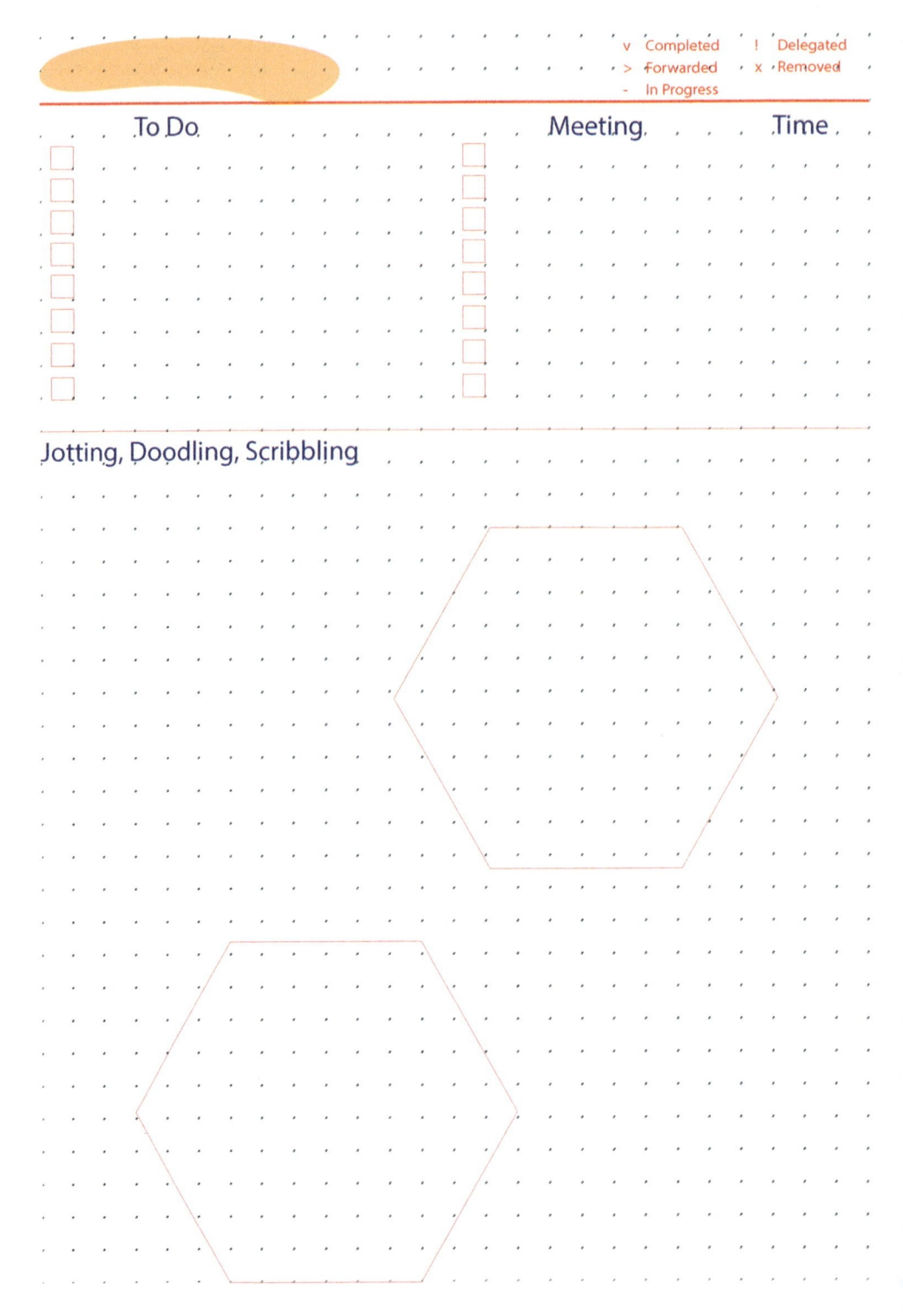

	v	Completed	!	Delegated
	>	Forwarded	x	Removed
	-	In Progress		

To Do   Meeting   Time

- [ ]
- [ ]
- [ ]
- [ ]
- [ ]
- [ ]
- [ ]
- [ ]
- [ ]

Jotting, Doodling, Scribbling

Daily Log

Weather	High		Sunny	Rainy
	Low		Partial Sunny	Snow
			Cloudy	

Reflections, Ideas, Diary

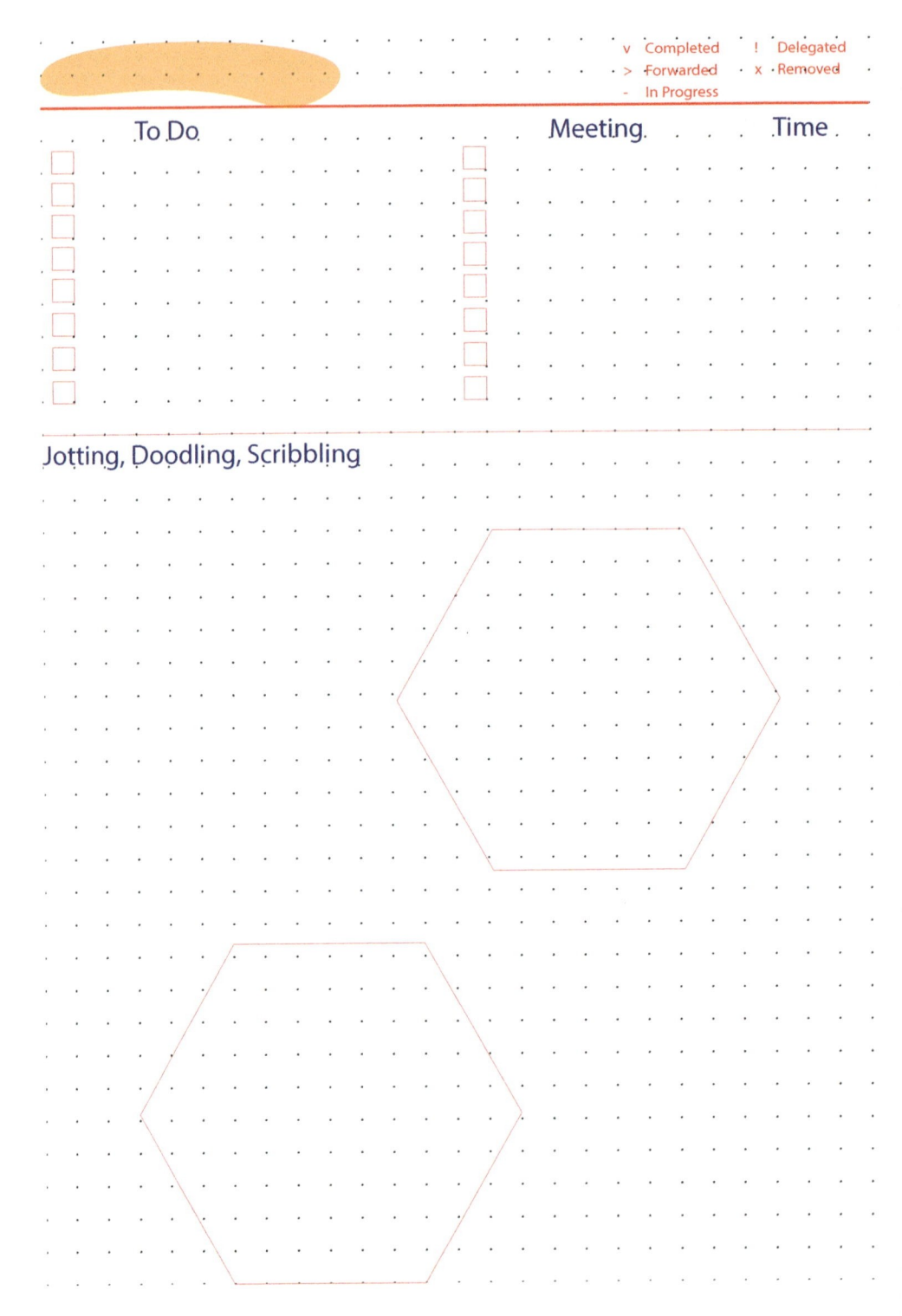

	v Completed	! Delegated
	> Forwarded	x Removed
	- In Progress	

To Do

☐
☐
☐
☐
☐
☐
☐
☐
☐
☐

Meeting

☐
☐
☐
☐
☐
☐
☐
☐

Time

Jotting, Doodling, Scribbling

Daily Log

Weather | High / Low | Sunny / Partial Sunny / Cloudy | Rainy / Snow

Reflections, Ideas, Diary

v Completed	! Delegated	
> Forwarded	x Removed	
- In Progress		

To Do

- [ ]
- [ ]
- [ ]
- [ ]
- [ ]
- [ ]
- [ ]
- [ ]
- [ ]
- [ ]

Meeting

- [ ]
- [ ]
- [ ]
- [ ]
- [ ]
- [ ]
- [ ]
- [ ]

Time

Jotting, Doodling, Scribbling

Daily Log

	Weather	High		Sunny	Rainy
		Low		Partial Sunny	Snow
				Cloudy	

Reflections, Ideas, Diary

Daily Log

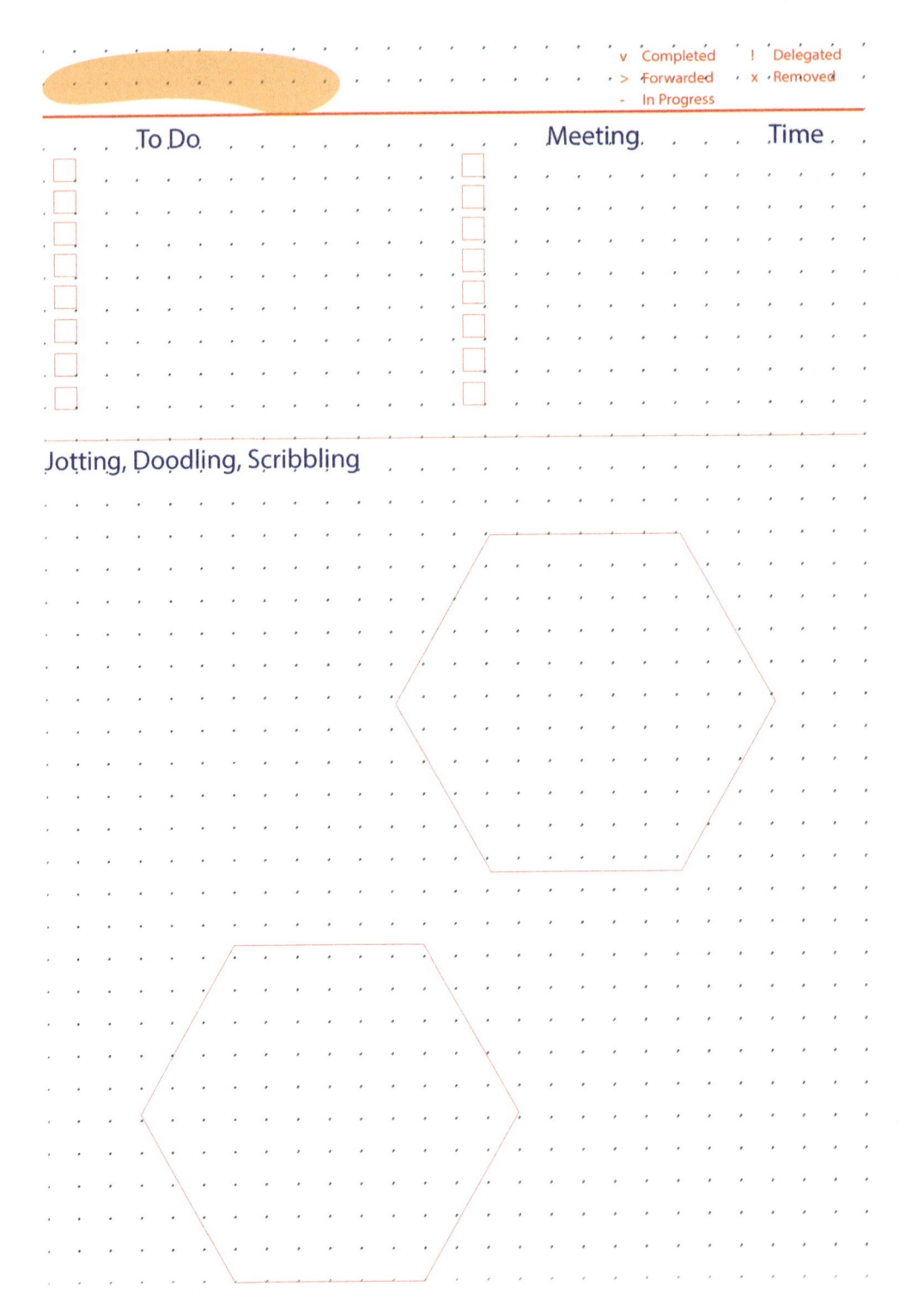

	v Completed	! Delegated
	> Forwarded	x Removed
	- In Progress	

To Do · Meeting · Time

☐
☐
☐
☐
☐
☐
☐
☐
☐

☐
☐
☐
☐
☐
☐
☐
☐
☐

Jotting, Doodling, Scribbling

Daily Log

Weather · High Sunny   Rainy
          Low   Partial Sunny Snow
                Cloudy

Reflections, Ideas, Diary

Daily Log   72

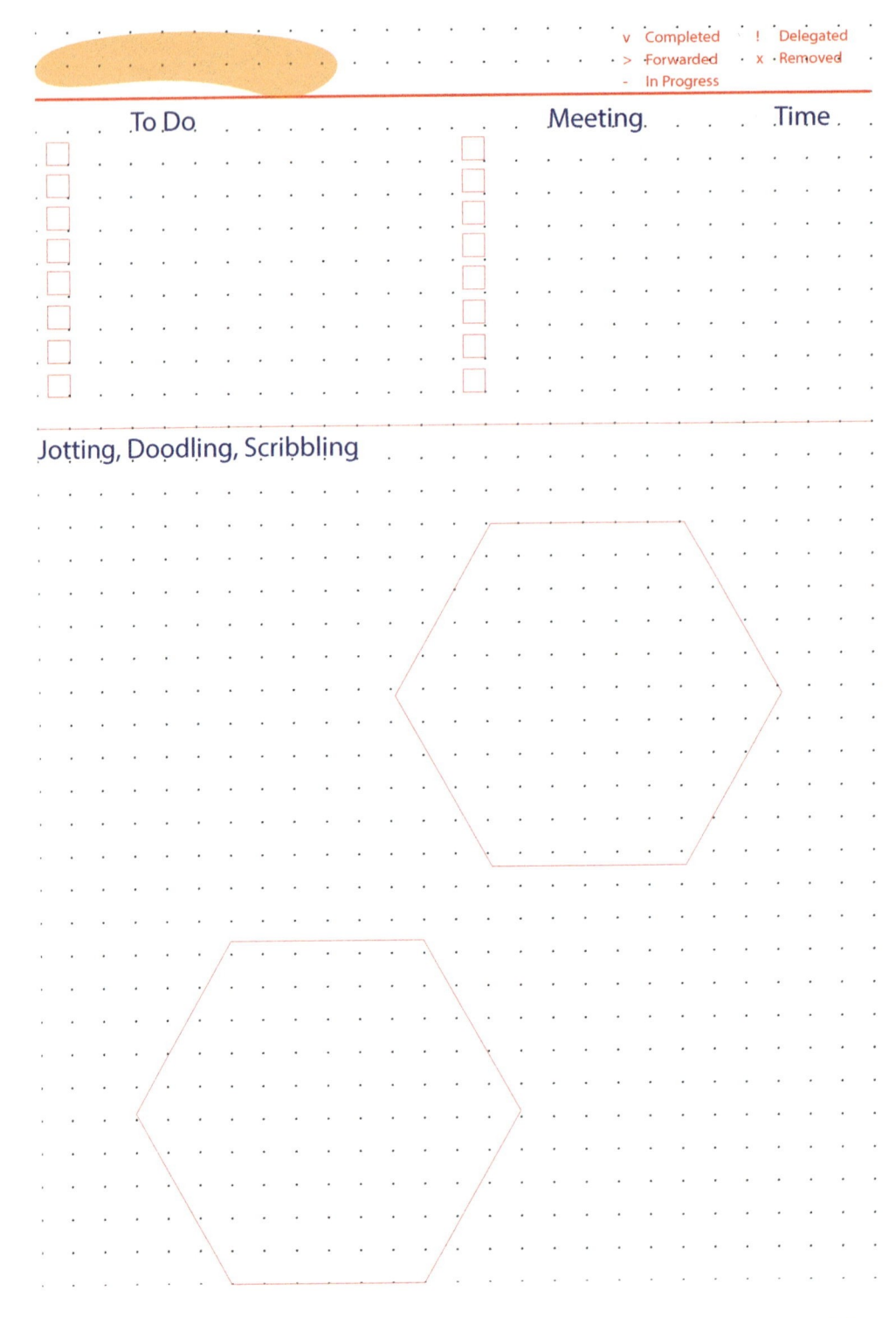

	Completed	!	Delegated
>	Forwarded	x	Removed
-	In Progress		

To Do   Meeting   Time

☐
☐
☐   ☐
☐   ☐
☐   ☐
☐   ☐
☐   ☐
☐   ☐
☐   ☐
☐   ☐
                            ☐

Jotting, Doodling, Scribbling

Daily Log

73

Weather · High / Low · Sunny / Partial Sunny / Cloudy · Rainy / Snow

Reflections, Ideas, Diary

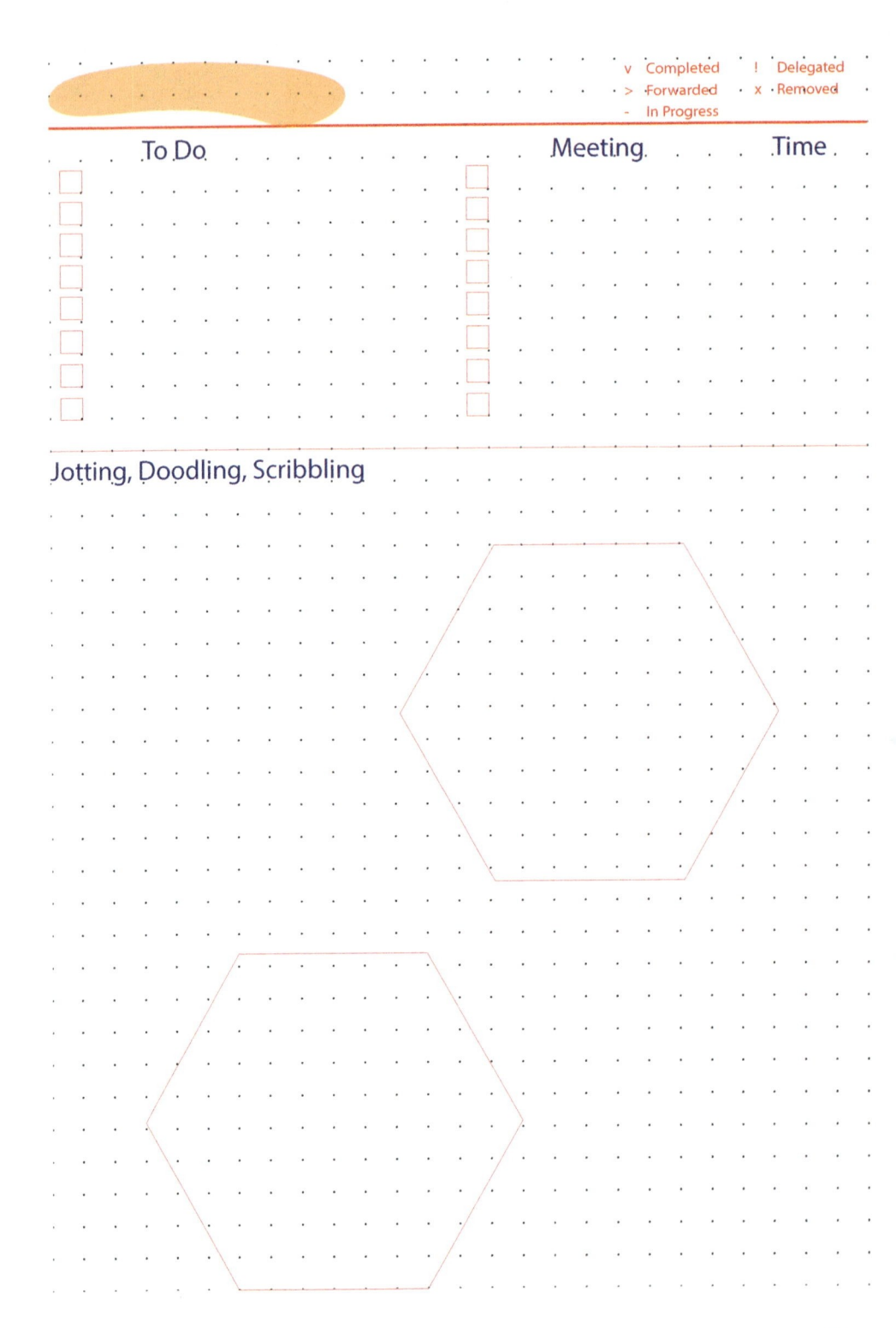

v Completed	! Delegated
> Forwarded	x Removed
- In Progress	

To Do   Meeting   Time

- [ ]   - [ ]
- [ ]   - [ ]
- [ ]   - [ ]
- [ ]   - [ ]
- [ ]   - [ ]
- [ ]   - [ ]
- [ ]   - [ ]
- [ ]   - [ ]
- [ ]

Jotting, Doodling, Scribbling

Daily Log

Weather | High / Low | Sunny · Partial Sunny · Cloudy | Rainy · Snow

Reflections, Ideas, Diary

Daily Log

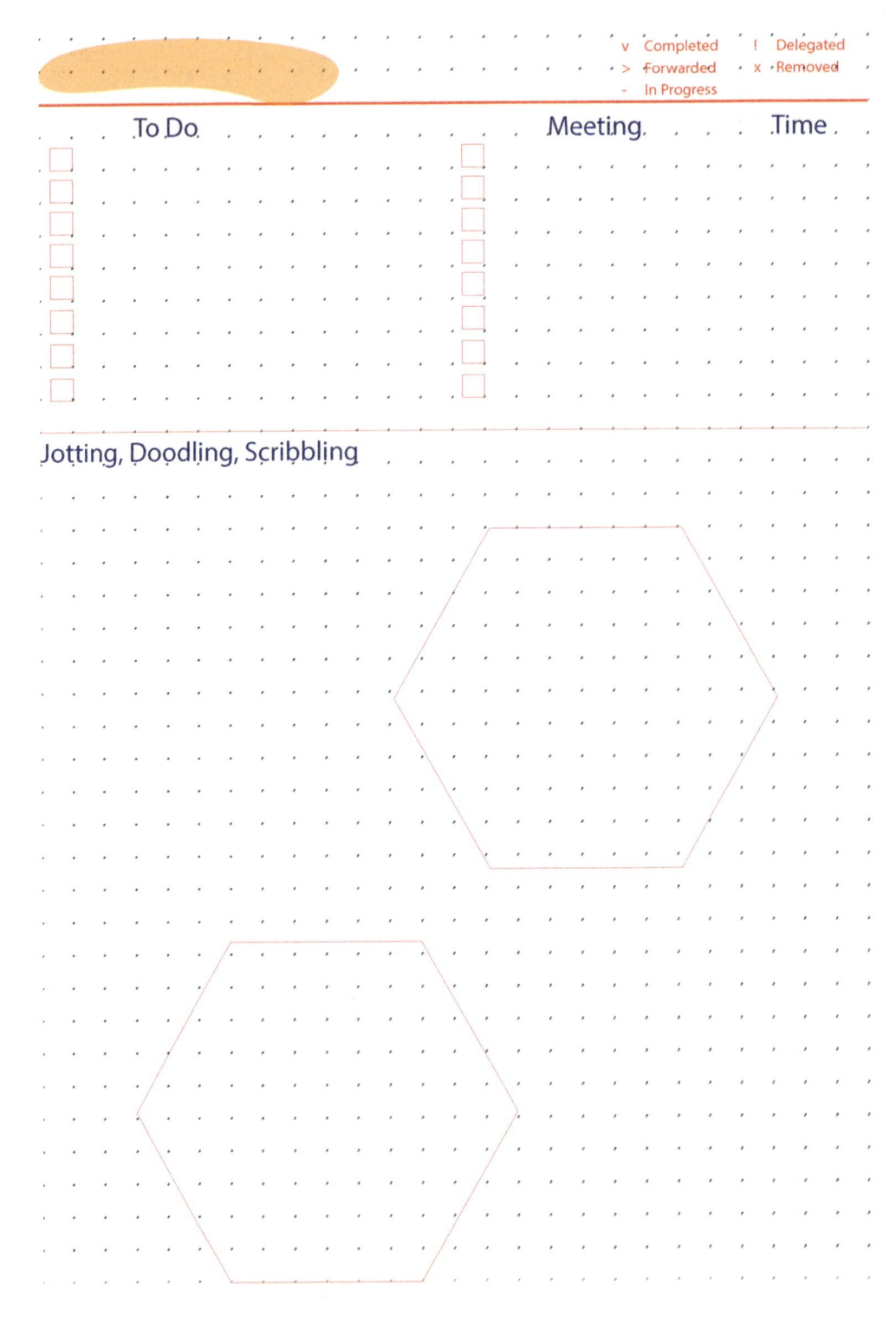

v Completed	! Delegated
> Forwarded	x Removed
- In Progress	

To Do

- [ ]
- [ ]
- [ ]
- [ ]
- [ ]
- [ ]
- [ ]
- [ ]
- [ ]
- [ ]

Meeting   Time

- [ ]
- [ ]
- [ ]
- [ ]
- [ ]
- [ ]
- [ ]
- [ ]
- [ ]
- [ ]

Jotting, Doodling, Scribbling

Daily Log

Weather	High		Sunny	Rainy
	Low		Partial Sunny	Snow
			Cloudy	

Reflections, Ideas, Diary

Made in the USA
Las Vegas, NV
12 February 2024